GW01375613

· A COMPENDIUM OF ·
HOUSEHOLD
HINTS

·A COMPENDIUM OF·
HOUSEHOLD
HINTS

by Charlotte Williams

A Compendium of Household Hints

This edition published in the UK in 2003 exclusively for
WHSmith Limited
Greenbridge Road
Swindon SN3 3LD
www.WHSmith.co.uk

by Toucan Books Ltd., London

Copyright Toucan Books Ltd. 2003

All rights reserved. No part of this book
may be reproduced, stored in a retrieval
system, or transmitted in any form or by
any means, electronic, electrostatic,
magnetic tape, mechanical, photocopying,
recording or otherwise, without permission
in writing from the publishers.

ISBN 1-903435-02-1

Cover illustration: Trina Dalziel
Author: Charlotte Williams
Additional text: Debbie Robertson
Cover design: Roy Williams
Page design: Joyce Mason
Managing editor: Ellen Dupont
Editor: Marion Dent
Designer: Vivian Foster
Picture researcher: Christine Vincent
Proofreader: Theresa Bebbington

The information in this book has been carefully researched and all efforts have been made to ensure its accuracy at the time of going to press. Toucan Books Ltd. and WHSmith Limited assume no responsibility for any injuries suffered or for damages or losses incurred during the use of or as a result of following this information. Read all directions carefully before taking any action based on the information and advice presented in this book. When using any commercial product, always read and follow label directions.

Cleanliness and order are not matters of instinct; they are matters of education, and like most great things, you must cultivate a taste for them.

Benjamin Disraeli (1804–1881)

Top Ten British Dog Names

	Male	Female
1	Sam	Trixie
2	Spot	Polly
3	Pip	Jessie
4	Duke	Lucy
5	Piper	Bonnie
6	Max	Cassie
7	Charlie	Daisy
8	Rocky	Heidi
9	Zak	Susie
10	Tiny	Holly

To Clean Blood From Clothing

A tiny speck of blood on clothing can be cleaned off by dabbing a small amount of saliva on it. Rub and repeat until the saliva dissolves the blood. This is a useful tip as an emergency measure if you are on the move. Once at home, soak in cold water, then wash with biological washing powder.

How to Make Banana Splits for Two

To make a chocolate sauce, melt *55g (2oz) of dark chocolate* in a saucepan over a low heat, or cook uncovered in a microwave for one to two minutes on full power. Stir in *60ml (4tbsp) of light corn syrup* and *60ml (4tbsp) of condensed milk*, and cook for a few minutes longer on the hob (or for 30 to 45 seconds in the microwave). Stir in *1.25ml (¼ tsp) of vanilla*. To assemble the banana splits, slice *one banana* lengthwise, place the halves at the bottom of a long, narrow sundae dish, then repeat for the second sundae. Put *three scoops of ice cream* along the centre of each of the split bananas. Spoon half of the warm sauce over the splits. Finally, add *whipped cream* and sprinkle *walnut pieces* on the top of the splits.

GIVING A COCKTAIL PARTY

THE PLAN

- Choose a style: classy and elegant? retro? fun and funky?
- Let your guests know whether dress is casual or more formal.
- Send out invitations. Be sure to include time, date and place.
- Add a few decorations to set the style for the party.
- Play cool, quiet music.
- Stand by the door and greet your guests.
- Mingle with your guests and introduce people to each other.
- Don't make the cocktails too strong. Because they can't taste the alcohol, people tend to drink quickly and may regret it later.
- Serve non-cocktail drinks too: wine, beer, soft drinks and sparkling water.
- Ask a friend to be responsible for mixing cocktails, or hire someone – you won't have time to do them all yourself.
- Serve canapés or finger foods with napkins.
- Keep an eye on the drink situation; put out more while the party is in full swing, then 'run out' when you want the party to end.

CLASSIC COCKTAILS

- *Gin*
  Gibson
  Gimlet
  Gin and Tonic
  Martini

- *Rum*
  Cuba Libre
  Daiquiri
  Mai Tai
  Planter's Punch

- *Tequilla*
  Cactus Bite
  Margarita
  Tequila Sunrise

- *Vodka*
  Bloody Mary
  Cosmopolitan
  Screwdriver

- *Champagne*
  Bellini
  Bucks Fizz
  Kir Royale

- *Bourbon*
  Kentucky Colonel
  Manhattan
  Mint Julep
  Old Fashioned

A COMPENDIUM OF HOUSEHOLD HINTS

Table Manners

Do

- Wait until your host sits down and asks you to start the meal.
- Break bread with your hands.
- Eat cheese by balancing a small portion on a piece of bread or biscuit.
- Swallow your food before talking.
- Be courteous to others.
- Compliment your hostess or host if you like your food.
- If a napkin ring is provided, fold your napkin and use it.

Don't

- Start to eat right away, unless asked to do so.
- Cut your bread with a knife.
- Eat cheese off your knife.
- Talk with your mouth full.
- Be obviously greedy.
- Make false compliments.
- Fold your napkin or leave it crumpled on your sideplate.

Belgian Beer . . .

Belgium is noted for its different types of beer. Five popular brews are:

Name	Description
Bacchus	a dark Flemish ale
Delirium tremens	a strong, blond beer
Judas	a golden ale
Kwak	an amber ale
Mort subite	a Gueuze Lambic beer

. . . and British Beer Glasses

Pilsner

A tall, elegant glass that is often used for drinking specialist, imported beers of different kinds.

Beer mug

A great British pub classic: solid glass mug with handle. Comes in 600ml (pint) and 300ml (half pint) sizes.

METRIC CONVERSIONS

LENGTH

1 millimetre (mm)	= 1,000 micrometres	= 0.0394 inch
1 centimetre (cm)	= 10 millimetres	= 0.3937 inch
1 metre (m)	= 100 centimetres	= 1.0936 yards
1 kilometre (km)	= 1,000 metres	= 0.6214 mile
1 inch (in)		= 2.54 centimetres
1 foot (ft)	= 12 inches	= 30.48 centimetres
1 yard (yd)	= 3 feet	= 0.9144 metre
1 mile (mi)	= 1,760 yards	= 1.6093 kilometres

AREA

1 sq centimetre	= 100 sq millimetres	= 01.55 sq inches
1 sq metre	= 10,000 sq centimetres	= 1.196 sq yards
1 hectare (ha)	= 10,000 sq metres	= 2.4711 acres
1 sq kilometre	= 100 hectares	= 0.3861 sq mile
1 sq foot	= 144 sq inches	= 0.0929 sq metre
1 sq yard	= 9 sq feet	= 0.8361 sq metre
1 acre (a)	= 4,840 sq yards	= 4,046.9 sq metres

CAPACITY

1 cu decimetre (dm)	= 1,000 cu centimetres	= 0.0353 cu foot
1 cu metre	= 1,000 cu decimetres	= 1.3080 cu yards
1 litre (l)	= 1 cu decimetre	= 0.22 gallon
1 cu yard	= 27 cu feet	= 0.7646 cu metre
1 pint (pt)	= 4 gills	= 0.5683 litre
1 gallon (gal)	= 8 pints	= 4.5461 litres

WEIGHT

1 gram (g)	= 1,000 milligrams	= 0.0353 ounce
1 kilogram (kg)	= 1,000 grams	= 2.2046 pounds
1 tonne (t)	= 1,000 kilograms	= 0.9842 ton
1 ounce (oz)	= 437.5 grains	= 28.350 grams
1 pound (lb)	= 16 ounces	= 0.4536 kilogram
1 stone (st)	= 14 pounds	= 6.3504 kilograms
1 ton (t)	= 2,204 pounds	= 1.0161 tonnes

A COMPENDIUM OF HOUSEHOLD HINTS

WINDOW CLEANING TIPS

- 👍 Make your own window cleaning solution by adding *30ml (2tbsp) of distilled malt vinegar* to warm water in a spray bottle. The vinegar dissolves greasy marks and makes the windows shine.
- 👍 Use crumpled newspaper to dry windows. The paper is very absorbent, and the ink helps to polish the glass to a shine.
- 👍 Wash windows on cloudy days. When they are slightly damp, you will be able to see every mark on them.
- 👍 Use horizontal strokes for polishing one side of the window and vertical on the other, so that you will be able to see which side any marks and smears are on.
- 👍 To get curtains out of the way without taking them down, hang a clothes hanger on the curtain rail. Then loop the curtain over it. Use one clothes hanger for each side of the window.
- 👍 In polluted areas, the outside surface of your windows will need to be cleaned regularly. The insides will need to be cleaned two or three times a year.
- 👍 Cut down on window cleaning by dusting your windows occasionally with a soft brush.

SOLUTION TO A STICKY PROBLEM

To get chewing gum out of a child's hair, rub peanut butter in well. Leave for 20 minutes, then comb through. The gum will come out, thanks to the oil in the peanut butter.

ONION SMELLS

If your hands smell after chopping onions, rub some mustard on them. Leave it on for a few minutes and then wash off.

DIMENSIONS OF BAKING CUTTERS, TINS, ETC.

3 mm	=	⅛ in
5 mm	=	¼ in
1 cm	=	½ in
2 cm	=	¾ in
2.5 cm	=	1 in
5 cm	=	2 in
6.5 cm	=	2½ in
7.5 cm	=	3 in
10 cm	=	4 in
15 cm	=	6 in
18 cm	=	7 in
20 cm	=	8 in
23 cm	=	9 in
25 cm	=	10 in
28 cm	=	11 in
30 cm	=	12 in
35 cm	=	14 in
40 cm	=	16 in

WHY THE GREGORIAN CALENDAR WORKS

The modern western calendar was introduced by Pope Gregory XIII (1502–85) in 1582 – ten years after he became pope. Keeping the seasons in line with any calendar system of fixed months and days is a problem because the Earth does not complete an orbit of the Sun (and a cycle of seasons) in a whole number of days – instead it takes 365.2422 days.

The Gregorian calendar takes this into account by inserting an extra day every four years, but omitting them in centennial years – unless the year is divisible by 400 (for example, 1900 was not a leap-year because it cannot be exactly divided by 400, but 2000, which has five 400s in it, was a leap-year). This gives an average year length of 365.2425 days, equivalent to just one day lost in 3,300 years.

A COMPENDIUM OF HOUSEHOLD HINTS

WASHING SYMBOLS

The number in the wash tub shows the most effective wash temperature in degrees C.

Hand wash only

IRON

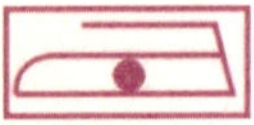

Cool iron 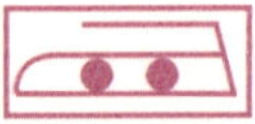 *Warm iron* 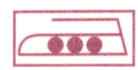 *Hot iron*

TUMBLE DRY

Low  *Medium*  *High*

DRY CLEAN

Standard  *Fluorine-solvent*  *Perchloreethylene*

DO NOT

Dry clean  *Tumble dry*  *Iron*  *Wash*

How to Stop Hiccups

There are many remedies for hiccups. Most of them involve ways of taking breath in or out so that the trapped air bubble causing the hiccup is dispersed.

- Suck a sugar lump.
- Swallow *5ml (1tsp) of vinegar*.
- Take a breath of air and 'swallow' it.
- Give the sufferer a fright, so that he or she breathes in sharply.
- Drink water from the wrong side of the glass. The lips should be on the side of the glass furthest away from the drinker, so that the water is drunk 'backwards'. (This can be messy.)

Silver Superstition

In a thunderstorm, put your silver away and take off silver jewellery. It may attract lightning.

Lipstick on Your Collar?

To get lipstick stains off a light-coloured garment first sprinkle bicarbonate of soda on to the stain. Then put the garment, stain side down, on to a large clean rag on your ironing board. Iron the fabric on the wrong side of the garment, using a hot iron. The heat will dissolve the grease in the lipstick and most or all of it will transfer to the rag.

Cleaning Blitz in a Laundry Basket

Unexpected guests need no longer present a threat to the untidy housewife! To clear up quickly, take a laundry basket and go from room to room picking up toys, clothes, books and anything else you find lying around in the way. Hide the basket in a cupboard and sort* through it later, once your guests have gone.

It is all too easy to put off sorting through the things in the laundry basket. The truly untidy would therefore do well not to own more than one laundry basket!

FIVE STEPS FOR PAINTING A ROOM

1 *Start with the ceiling*
If using a brush, avoid drips from the ceiling by pushing the handle of the brush through a paper plate before you start. If using a roller, make sure you don't put on too much paint or it will drip.

2 *Walls*
When painting walls, start at the top. To avoid brush marks, paint horizontally and then vertically, overlapping your sections.

3 *Doors*
If using gloss paint, open windows to release the fumes. Shut the door while painting the back of it, working downwards, then open it until the paint is dry. Last of all, paint the door frame.

4 *Windows*
Start this job early in the day so windows can be closed by nightfall. Stick masking tape on the glass along the edges of the frames so you don't paint the glass, then remove the tape when the paint is dry.

5 *Skirting boards*
Hold a piece of cardboard against the top of the skirting board (or behind pipes if painting them in a contrasting colour), to stop the paint from going on to the walls.

SN'EASY DOES IT!

Keep pets off furniture by sprinkling pepper on the fabric. Hoover up the specks and renew every few days. Stop puppies chewing furniture legs by wiping a cloth dampened with oil of cloves over the wood, or spray furniture with cheap whisky. They will hate the smell and taste.

SOOTY STAINS

If soot falls on to your carpet from the fireplace, the best way to deal with it is to sprinkle it with salt, then wait for two hours before vacuuming it up.

> ### Bread
>
> TO FRESHEN STALE BREAD
> Run some cold water over it very briefly, just so as to dampen it slightly, then wrap in foil. Put it in a hot oven for five to ten minutes, being careful not to let it burn. It will come up soft and fresh every time.

Ecological Bleach

As an ecological alternative to bleach, mix *75ml (2fl oz) of distilled malt vinegar* with *75ml (2fl oz) of lemon juice*. Add *4.5l (1gal) or so of warm water* and soak white fabrics for a quarter of an hour before putting them in the washing machine.

How to Make a Mai Tai Cocktail

Coat the rim of a cocktail glass with *one egg white*, lightly beaten, then dip the edge in *sugar*. Mix up equal parts of *white rum, orange juice* and *lime juice* with *3 crushed ice cubes*. Pour liquid (including ice cubes) into the glass and garnish with *cherries* and *pineapple cubes*.

Cleaning Mirrors

Never spray water on to a mirror to clean it. The water seeps around the edges of the mirror and makes dark spots on it. Instead, clean the mirror with a soft cloth, moistened with a solution of half distilled malt vinegar and half water. To finish off, polish the mirror with a dry cloth.

SOAKING AND COOKING TIMES OF DRIED BEANS AND PULSES

Variety of pulse	Soaking	Boiling	Simmering
Aduki beans	4 hr	10 min	1–1½ hr
Black beans	4 hr	10 min	1–2 hr
Black-eyed beans	4 hr	10 min	1–1½ hr
Borlotti beans	4 hr	10 min	1–1½ hr
Broad beans	4 hr	10 min	1–2 hr
Brown beans	4 hr	10 min	1–2 hr
Butter beans	4 hr	10 min	1–2 hr
Cannellini beans	4 hr	10 min	1½–2 hr
Chickpeas	8 hr	10 min	2–3 hr
Field beans	8 hr	10 min	2–3 hr
Flageolet beans	4 hr	10 min	1½–2 hr
Haricot beans	4 hr	10 min	1–1½ hr
Lentils – brown	None	None	½–1 hr
– green	None	None	½–1 hr
– Puy	None	None	½–1 hr
– red	None	None	20–30 min
Lima beans	4 hr	10 min	1–1½ hr
Mung beans	4 hr	10 min	½–1 hr
Navy beans	4 hr	10 min	1–1½ hr
Peas – split	1 hr		¾–1 hr
– whole	4 hr	10 min	1–1½ hr
Pinto beans	4 hr	10 min	1–2 hr
Red kidney beans	4 hr	10 min	1–2 hr
Soya beans	8 hr	1 hr	2–4 hr

CONVERTING KCAL TO KJOULES

$$1 \text{ kcal} = 4.184 \text{ kJ}$$

For ease of calculation, round up to 4.2.

For example, to find how many Kjoules are in an apple that has 50 calories, multiply 50 x 4.2 to get 210kJ.

Do's and Don'ts of Conversation

Conversation should arise naturally out of the situation, but sometimes we are forced to direct it. Do not feel embarrassed about having little to say; quiet people are often better company than everlasting talkers. At the same time, make an effort to say something, otherwise you may appear rude or bored.

Do

- Discuss current events.
- Take an interest in what others have to say.
- Listen as well as speak.
- Praise achievements of others, with sincerity.
- Ask general questions about a person's health, occupation and so on.
- Remember other people are not as interested in your children as you are.
- Talk about your work in general terms.
- Find common interests or subjects that will interest everyone present.
- Leave a gap for quiet, shy people to speak.

Don't

- Talk about the weather, unless it's the only topic.
- Contradict other people's strong opinions.
- Make catty remarks.
- Emphasise your own abilities or achievements.
- Ask intrusive personal questions: it's not an interrogation!
- Discuss your ailments.
- Talk about your work in detail; it's boring.
- Talk for the sake of talking. Silence is better than incessant chatter.
- Interrupt when someone else is talking.

A COMPENDIUM OF HOUSEHOLD HINTS

DARN IT!
Darns are usually worked on the wrong side of the fabric, using a running stitch. You will need:
- an assortment of wools, silks, cottons and needles
- thimble and small scissors
- a darning 'mushroom' (don't strain fabric over this device when you are darning, otherwise your darn will bulge out when it is removed).

> Look at the size of the hole.

> Start your darn well away from the hole, on sound fabric, otherwise the darn will not last.

> Choose a thread similar in colour and weight to the fabric, and a needle of the right size.

> Darn in and out across the hole using double thread or wool; make short stitches either side of the hole and long ones across it.

> Use double thread, but don't knot the end.

> Loose threads and tears from the fabric can also be worked in to the darn, to make it stronger.

> When you have run your stitches across the hole vertically, which is the first stage, move to the second stage.

> Run your stitches across the hole horizontally, in and out of the vertical threads you have made, as though you were weaving.

TREAT YOUR HANDS WITH KID GLOVES

For beautiful hands, sleep with an old pair of chamois leather gloves on. This will help to make your hands soft.

HAYBOX COOKERY

Cooking food in a hay box is a marvellous way to save fuel. First, bring the contents of a pan to boil, then pack it away in the box filled with hay. It will continue to cook in its own heat; hay does not conduct heat, so the heat does not escape.

LEMON FRESH

If you squeeze lemon juice over a stained wooden table top or breadboard and leave it overnight, it will clean up beautifully.

EGGS IS EGGS

- Put an egg in a pan of cold water. If it stands up, it is not fresh. If it lies flat, it is.

- When you break a fresh egg into a dish, the yolk should be rounded, and the white should be flat and jelly-like.

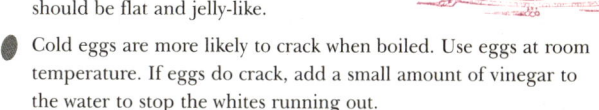

- Cold eggs are more likely to crack when boiled. Use eggs at room temperature. If eggs do crack, add a small amount of vinegar to the water to stop the whites running out.

- If an egg is stuck to the carton, use a little water to wet the box and it will come off easily.

- Keep a separate saucepan for boiling eggs. Dirty shells can be a health hazard.

- The cooled-down boiled water can be used to water houseplants. It contains valuable nutrients for plants.

- Whisk egg whites in a clean bowl with no traces of butter or any other fat. Fat will stop the eggs whisking properly.

A COMPENDIUM OF HOUSEHOLD HINTS

Cotton Fabrics and Their Care

Cotton comes in many different styles of fabric and is often mixed with other fibres, so always check the care instructions before washing.

- Pure white cotton can be boiled to keep it white.
- Colourfast cottons can go in a hot wash but may still bleed a little.
- Non-colourfast cottons should be washed on a warm wash to prevent colours running.

Fabric	Use/Appearance	Care
Calico	An undyed fabric with a slightly rough texture	Wash as for colourfast cotton
Cambric	Fine fabric with a smooth, slightly stiff appearance	Wash according to colour
Canvas	A strong fabric with a rough finish, often used for bags and upholstery	Scrub with detergent and warm water
Corduroy	Hardwearing and warm, usually made from cotton	Do not wring; iron on wrong side while still damp
Denim	Hardwearing but tends to shrink in the wash; colour often fades patchily	Wash as for non-colourfast cotton
Drill	Durable, raised surfac	Wash according to colour
Gabardine	Often treated with a water-resistant finish for rainwear.	Dry clean only
Poplin	Cotton or mixed fabric with a smooth, crisp finish	Wash according to fibre type
Sailcloth	Strong, stiff pure or mixed fabric	Wash according to fibre type
Seersucker	Has a crinkly finish and is often printed in brightly coloured stripes	Wash as for colourfast cotton unless otherwise instructed; do not iron

Packing Clothes

If you want to avoid creasing your clothes when travelling, roll rather than fold them into your suitcase. Lay several garments, one on top of another, in a neat pile. Then, starting at one end, roll them all carefully into one bundle. Put the bundle in the centre of your suitcase. You can put underwear, socks and small items around it, but try not to put heavy items on top of it. When you reach your destination, take out the roll and hang each garment up immediately. You will find that the rolled-up clothes will not need ironing.

Oversalted Foods

If you have mistakenly oversalted food, for example, by boiling down a stew with salty bacon in it, there are various ways you can rescue the dish. For stews and soups, you can add a raw potato, then boil. Discard the potato, which will have absorbed most of the salt. For vegetables, pour on boiled water, which will rinse away surface salt. After rinsing, over-salted boiled potatoes can be mashed with milk and an egg.

Beating Creases

Clothes that have dried out completely may have creases that are difficult to iron away. One way to dampen the clothes is to put them into a tumble dryer for a few minutes with a wet towel. Run the dryer on the 'no heat' setting.

Ways to Fight Fleas

- Fumigation with brimstone.
- Sprinkle sheets, upholstery, clothing, carpets and curtains with essence of peppermint.
- Sew fresh leaves of penny royal in a bag and leave it on the bed, or wherever else you have a flea problem.

Say it with Flowers

From earliest times, country people used images of flowers, fruits and leaves to express emotions between lovers, friends and family. Folk songs, poems and sayings are full of these ancient metaphors, which are often linked with the passage of the seasons in the countryside. In the eighteenth and nineteenth centuries, upper-class ladies began to use 'the language of flowers' to send coded messages to their suitors and friends.

Flower/fruit/leaf	Meaning	Flower/fruit/leaf	Meaning
Anemone	Unfading love	*Magnolia*	Perseverance
Acorn	Immortality	*Marigold*	Heart's comfort
Bluebell	Humility	*Mistletoe*	Kiss me
Daisy	Innocence	*Oak leaf*	Fertility
Forget-me-not	True love	*Pansy*	Thought
Four-leaf clover	Luck	*Periwinkle*	Fond remembrance
Foxglove	Insincerity		
Honeysuckle	Generous affection	*Poppy*	Health and success
Holly	Good will	*Primrose*	Young love
Hollyhock	Female ambition	*Red rose bud*	Pure and lovely
Iris	Faith	*Rue*	Disdain
Ivy	Friendship	*Sweet Pea*	Farewell
Jasmine	Elegance	*Sweet William*	Gallantry
Lilac	First love	*Violet*	Modesty
Lily	Purity	*White rose*	True worth
Lily-of-the-valley	Sweetness	*Willow*	Inconstancy

WOOLLEN FABRICS AND THEIR CARE

Wool is a warm fibre from the fleece of a sheep.

- Always check the care instructions on the label in a woollen garment. When mixed with synthetic fabrics, some woollens can be washed in a machine. If in doubt, dry clean.
- Pure wool must be handwashed and rinsed in cool water, to avoid shrinking. Never soak or bleach wool.
- Do not wring, but wrap in a towel and squeeze the water out. Dry flat away from heat, with proper ventilation.

Fabric	Use/Appearance	Care
Angora	Fluffy wool with rabbit fur	Wash as for wool
Bouclé	Fabric with a thick, bobbly surface made up of curls or loops woven from a variety of fibres, especially wool	Usually needs to be dry cleaned
Flannel	An old-fashioned fabric with many different finishes	Wash carefully as for wool, or dry clean
Jersey	A knitted, stretchy fabric made from fine wool	Wash following care instructions, or dry clean
Mohair	Fibre from the angora goat	Wash as for wool; do not let the fabric felt up
Serge	A strong, hardwearing fabric originally made from wool and used for uniforms. Now mixed with synthetic fabrics to give it longer life	Dry clean only
Tweed	Used for making suits, skirts and coats, now sometimes woven from synthetic fibres	Dry cleaning is safest

A COMPENDIUM OF HOUSEHOLD HINTS

FOR A DELICIOUS CUP OF TEA

- Use good quality leaf tea. Look for brands with identifiable leaves, and a fresh, bracing scent.
- Mix your teas to create your own special blend. China teas can add light, refreshing flavours to strong, pungent Indian teas.
- Use a teapot. Making tea with a teabag and boiling water in the cup may be quick, but the tea will never taste as good.
- Warm the teapot before you make the tea. Pour in a small amount of hot water and rinse it around the pot before tipping it out.
- Add tea: 'One for each person and one for the pot' is the traditional rule.
- Teabags can make excellent tea if you use a pot, but purists prefer to make tea with loose tea leaves.
- Use freshly boiled water, rather than water that has already been boiled several times. It helps to oxygenate the tea and improves the taste.
- Make sure the water is boiling when you pour it on to the teabags or tea leaves. If the water is not boiling, the tea will not infuse properly and will taste unpleasant.
- Leave the tea to stand for several minutes before pouring a cup. The stronger you like your tea, the longer you should leave it to infuse.
- To speed up the process of infusion, open the top of the teapot and press the teabags gently with a teaspoon.
- Do not let tea stand so long that it cools. If this happens, it will taste 'stewed' and bitter.
- Add milk and sugar to taste. Some people prefer their milk poured in before the tea, some after.
- For black tea (with no milk), add a slice of lemon to stop scum forming on the surface of the tea in hard water areas.
- For the best taste, drink tea out of a china cup and saucer or a china mug.

Sit down and relax to drink your tea so that you can fully savour what Mrs Beeton called 'the cup that cheers but does not inebriate'.

HEALTHY LIVING

The essentials of healthy living are:
1. A balanced diet.
2. Plenty of exercise and fresh air.
3. Adequate rest and sleep.
4. Personal hygiene.
5. Avoidance of any focus of infection.

RESCUE A BURNT PAN

A burnt pan can be cleaned by filling it with hot water and adding *15ml (1tbsp) of bicarbonate of soda or biological washing powder*. Leave it to soak for half an hour, and the burnt food should come off easily when you clean the pan.

WEDDING ANNIVERSARIES

Year	*Material*
Tenth	Tin
Fifteenth	Crystal
Twentieth	China
Twenty-fifth	Silver
Thirtieth	Pearl
Thirty-fifth	Coral
Fortieth	Ruby
Forty-fifth	Sapphire
Fiftieth	Gold
Fifty-fifth	Emerald
Sixtieth	Diamond

RESTRINGING A NECKLACE

If you need to restring a broken necklace, use nylon fishing line. The line is rigid enough to use without threading it through a needle. It is also very tough and is unlikely to break.

A COMPENDIUM OF HOUSEHOLD HINTS

BABY FINGERNAILS

The easiest way to trim a baby's fingernails is to bite the excess nail away with your teeth. Babies' fingernails are thin and come away easily. They are also very small, so if you choose to use nail scissors only use a pair specially designed for a baby – preferably when your baby is asleep (scissors might cause an accident if an awake baby moved suddenly).

FIRST AID FOR TIGHTS

Paint small holes or ladders in tights with clear nail polish. It will stop them from getting any bigger.

HOW TO PRONOUNCE SOME TRICKY SURNAMES

Spelt	Pronounced
Bagshot	Baggot
Beauchamp	Beecham
Beaulieu	Bewley
Belvoir	Beever
Berkeley	Barkley
Bourchier	Boucher
Brougham	Broom
Cholmondely	Chumley
Cirencester	Sissester
Claverhouse	Clavers
Cockburn	Coburn
Cowper	Coope
Dalziel	Dale
Drogheda	Droida
Featherstonehaugh	Fanshaw
Fiennes	Fines

Spelt	Pronounced
Greenwich	Grinnidge
Grosvenor	Grovenor
Hawarden	Harden
Holborn	Hoburn
Home	Hume
Macleod	Macloud
Mainwaring	Mannering
Marjoribanks	Marshbanks
Menzies	Mingis
Norwich	Norridge
Plaistow	Plaastow
Salisbury	Saulsbury
St Clair	Sincler
St John	Sinjon
Strachan	Strawn
Worcester	Wooster

Some surnames are pronounced differently by different families: for example, Pepys *can be pronounced* Peppis, Peeps *or* Pips.

Top Ten British Cat Names

1 Sooty
2 Tigger
3 Lucy
4 Smokey
5 Charlie
6 Smudge
7 Thomas
8 Sam
9 Misty
10 Lucky

To Stop Static From Tights

If your skirt clings to your tights, put some hand lotion on your hands and then rub your hands over your tights while you are wearing them. If your tights are black, rub the lotion in well so that it doesn't show up against the dark colour. You will find that the lotion smooths the tights, so that when you put your skirt or dress on, the fabric will not cling to them.

How to Make a Harvey Wallbanger Cocktail

Crack *4–5 ice cubes* and put into a cocktail shaker with *37.5ml (1¼fl oz) vodka* and *90ml (3fl oz) orange juice*. Shake well and pour into a highball glass and float *15ml (½fl oz) Galliano* on the top.

Make your own Deer Repellent

To keep deer out of your garden, mix *20 raw eggs* into *4.5l (1gal) of water*. Spray on to bushes, shrubs and trees up to a height of 1.5m (5ft). You won't notice the smell, but the deer will hate it and stay away. You will need to spray again after heavy rain. Dried blood fertiliser will also keep deer at bay.

Painting and Decorating Terms

Emulsion
Water-based paint. Easy to work with. Low odour. Available in matt or satin. Drips or smudges of emulsion can be wiped off quickly, and brushes can be cleaned easily in cold water.

Gloss
Strong-smelling, hardwearing oil-based paint. Use on window frames, skirting boards and picture rails. Apply in a well-ventilated room. Clean brushes with white spirit.

Paint kettle
A small container for paint. Pour small amounts of paint from the can into your paint kettle as you do the job.

Primer
A type of paint used to seal porous surfaces such as wood and unpainted plaster, to make them ready for painting.

Roller
A piece of sponge or fabric on a roller with a handle, used for covering the large surfaces of walls or ceilings. Radiator rollers are designed to fit behind radiators, and are small with long handles.

Textured paint
Thick paint with a rough finish, used to hide cracks or bumps in a wall.

Undercoat
A base coat. Ensures that the previous colour will not show through in the top coat. Also ensures final coat will be opaque and smooth.

Vinyl
Paint with slight sheen. Easy to wipe clean. For kitchens or bathrooms.

CHOPPING WOOD SAFELY

To chop wood, make sure you place the hand holding the wood in the right position; in this way, you are more likely to be safe rather than sorry.

Incorrect   *Correct*

HOUSEHOLD ADAGES

The devil makes work for idle hands.

It's no use crying over spilt milk.

Red sky at night, shepherd's delight
(it will be fine enough to put out washing to dry);
red sky in the morning, shepherd's warning
(it will rain and washing should not be put out).

A stitch in time saves nine.

Take care of the pennies and the pounds will take care of themselves.

Too many cooks spoil the broth.

You can't make a silk purse out of a sow's ear.

You can't teach an old dog new tricks.

Work expands to fit the time available.

SHELLFISH

Never eat shellfish when there's no R in the month: May, June, July and August.

CARVING TIPS
Carving beef, lamb or pork
- Use a sharp knife, sharpened on a steel before you start.
- Use a large carving fork with long prongs, in order to hold the meat steady while you carve.
- Make sure your portions are of equal size.
- Carve a sirloin of beef by starting with the thickest part of the meat.

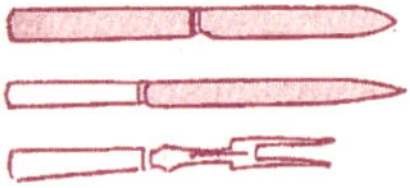

Carving chickens, ducks and turkeys
- Remove legs and wings of a bird first.
- Make sure each guest has an equal amount of leg, wing and breast.

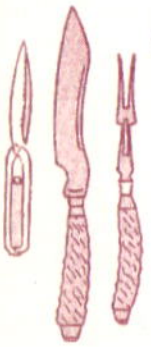

Carving game
- Use special game carvers and game scissors, rather than trying to cut tough game with a knife.

Carving ham
- Cut ham on a slant, and remember to hold the meat in position using a large carving fork.

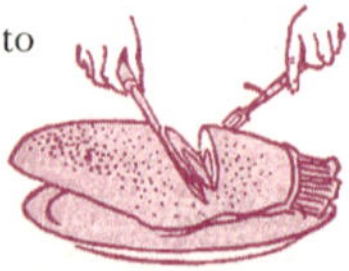

Serving fish
- Cut a large fish such as a salmon into thick slices to make fish steaks.
- Cut flat fish down the backbone, so that you can flake the slices off easily from either side. 
- Use a silver knife rather than a steel knife for fish. Alternatively, use a silver fish slice.

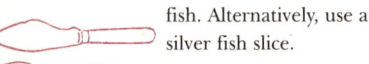

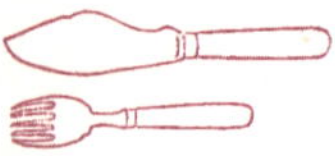

BIRTHSTONES

Month	Stone	Colour	Meaning
JANUARY	Garnet	Red	Constancy
FEBRUARY	Amethyst	Purple	Sincerity
MARCH	Bloodstone or Aquamarine	Green/red or Blue	Courage
APRIL	Diamond	White/clear	Innocence
MAY	Emerald	Green	Love and success
JUNE	Pearl, Alexandrite or Moonstone	Cream	Health and longevity
JULY	Ruby	Red	Contentment
AUGUST	Sardonyx or Peridot	Light green	Married happiness
SEPTEMBER	Sapphire	Blue	Clear thinking
OCTOBER	Opal or Tourmaline	Many colours	Hope
NOVEMBER	Topaz	Yellow/brown	Fidelity
DECEMBER	Turquoise or Lapis Lazuli	Blue	Prosperity

A COMPENDIUM OF HOUSEHOLD HINTS

POMADE MADE EASY
For reasons that may become clear if you follow this recipe, pomade has gone out of fashion since Mrs. Beeton's time. She recommended mixing *112.5g (¼lb) of lard* with *two pennyworth of castor oil*, then adding *a few drops of scent* and put the pomade into pots. She exhorts readers to tighten the lids, to stop the pomade going rancid.

HOW TO DRY THE INSIDE OF A DECANTER
With its narrow neck and bulbous bottom, it is impossible to dry the inside of a decanter with a tea towel. Leaving it upside down to drip is unsatisfactory. The arrangement is unstable and drips will leave marks on the clean glass. However, you can achieve perfect results by taking your cleaned decanter and filling it to the brim with cold water. Then, under a running cold tap, turn the decanter upside down – all the water, including any drops, will rush out. Hold the decanter under the running water for a few more seconds. Then remove it and turn off the tap. Turn the decanter right side up and dry the outside and any drips that remain around the lip. Now your decanter will be dry and sparkling.

PULLING OUT NAILS
If you need to pull nails out of a wooden surface, put a thin wood block between the hammer head and the surface. This will stop the head from making dents and splinters in the wooden surface, and it also helps to lever out the nail.

THE HAND MIRROR TEST
To detect damp in a bed, put a hand mirror between the sheets for a few minutes. If the glass turns misty, you will know the bed is damp.

HOW TO SMOKE A CIGAR

- For beginners, the recommendation is usually to start on a long, thin cigar, because it is less likely to cause an embarrassing fit of unseemly coughing and choking. Small, fat cigars are very strong and overpowering.
- When selecting a cigar you should inspect it to make sure there are no lumps and that the paper is not discoloured. These often indicate low quality.
- Tap the blade of your cutter against the cigar, to ensure it is perfectly positioned. Cut the cigar where the cap meets the wrapper. Then cut horizontally in one slice.
- If possible, light your cigar with a cigar lighter (it's designed to produce a longer flame than a cigarette lighter). If you have to use matches, use a long one – and wait until the sulphur burns away before smoking the cigar.
- Remove the band while smoking the cigar. Once the cigar is lit, the band does not need to be there; its only purpose is to stop the tobacco tearing.
- Do not inhale the cigar smoke.

CAPACITY OF BAKING PANS, BOWLS, TINS, ETC.

300ml	=	½pt
450ml	=	¾pt
600ml	=	1pt
900ml	=	1½pt
1 litre	=	2pt
1.25 litres	=	2½pt
1.5 litres	=	3pt
2 litres	=	3½pt
2.5 litres	=	5pt
3.5 litres	=	7pt

A COMPENDIUM OF HOUSEHOLD HINTS

COOKING TEMPERATURES

Description	°C	°F	Gas mark
Very low	140	275	1
Low	150–170	300–325	1–3
Moderate	180–190	350–375	4–5
Hot	200	400	6–7
Very hot	220–260	425–475	8–9

Long-life Bread
When making bread dough, use water that you have boiled potatoes in. This helps to keep the bread fresher for longer.

The Etiquette of Gloves
When making afternoon calls, ladies should not remove their gloves. If they do, their hostess may fear that they are planning to make a long stay.

Colour-fast Art
To stop colours from rubbing off a child's painting or drawing, simply fix them with hairspray. The hairspray will also make the paper stiffer and your child's artwork will last longer.

The Drinker's Dilemma
Worried about mixing your drinks? Remember the adage: Wine before beer makes you feel queer; beer before wine makes you feel fine. Sober heads, however, counsel moderation above all.

COMPOSITION OF CHOCOLATE

This table gives the composition of different types of chocolate.

Type of chocolate	Chocolate liquor* %	Added cocoa butter %	Sugar %	Milk solids %
Bitter	95	5	0	0
Bittersweet	35–50	15	50–35	0
Sweet	15	15	70	0
Milk	10	20	50	15

Chocolate liquor is the term for the thick liquid made from the roasted and ground kernels of the cocoa bean (the nibs). It is more than half cocoa butter.

ENGAGEMENT RINGS

The tradition of the engagement ring dates back to the days when marriage was a financial transaction. In ancient times, gold rings were used as a kind of currency. A man would offer his bride a gold ring, signifying a partial payment as well as his intentions. However, Roman brides wore iron rings as a symbol of the unbreakable nature of their marital bond.

CARE OF VELVET

Good quality velvet is an expensive, luxurious fabric used for curtains and clothing.

- Do not iron velvet: it is better to steam the crushed pile.
- Cotton and silk velvets should be dry cleaned.
- Synthetic velvet can be washed according to care instructions.
- Lighter, more flexible velour is often made from synthetic fibres.

A COMPENDIUM OF HOUSEHOLD HINTS

CHOOSING DIAMONDS: THE 4 CS

CUT
The main diamond cuts:

marquise

oval

emerald   *princess*   *radiant*

pear   *round brilliant*

heart

COLOUR
Diamonds are found in all colours including black but most diamonds are yellowish. This list ranks these diamonds in order of desirability and assigns each a letter.

Letters correspond to colour values:

D pure white

E exceptional white

F excellent white

G good white

H white

I slightly tinted white

J commercial white

K tinted white

L tinted white, set in yellow

M champagne

N yellowish champagne

O yellowish

P yellowish tinted

CLARITY

Almost all diamonds have small flaws, called inclusions. The fewer inclusions, the greater the clarity.

If no inclusions, internally flawless

VVS1 very very small inclusions, pin pricks

VVS2 very very small inclusions, pin pricks

VS1 very small, still minute

VS2 very small, still minute

S11 tiny

S12 tiny

I1 small, difficult to recognise to naked eye

I2 larger and/or more inclusions, recognisable to naked eye

I3 larger and/or more inclusions, recognisable to naked eye

CARAT

Diamond weights are measured in carats. A carat equals 0.2gm (0.0070502oz) and has 100 points.

Weight (ct)	Size (diam.)	Weight: (pt)
0.05ct	1.00mm	5pt
0.10ct	3.00mm	10pt
0.20ct	3.85mm	20pt
0.25ct	4.10mm	25pt
0.33ct	4.55mm	33pt
0.40ct	4.80mm	40pt
0.50ct	5.15mm	50pt
0.66ct	5.72mm	66pt
0.75ct	6.00mm	75pt
0.90ct	6.40mm	90pt
1.00ct	6.65mm	100pt

KNOW YOUR ALPHABET

GIA – Gemological Institute of America
GTL – Gem Testing Laboratory of Great Britain
HRD – Diamond High Council, Antwerp

HERBS

Just as flowers have a language, herbs too have hidden meanings. Some are ancient, others were adopted by the Victorians. Shakespeare often used the language of herbs in his plays.

Herb	Meaning
Allspice	Compassion
Aloe	Grief
Angelica	Inspiration
Aniseed	Restoration of youth
Bay leaf	Strength
Borage	Courage
Calendula	Joy
Cinnamon	My fortune is yours
Fennel	Praiseworthy
Juniper	Protection
Lavender	Devotion
Lemon balm	Bringing love
Marjoram	Joy and happiness
Rosemary	Remembrance
Sage	Wisdom
Thyme	Affection

TO PREPARE A FLOOR FOR A DANCE

The floor should be swept and scrubbed and then, when dry, well sprinkled with powdered boric acid, which should be rubbed in thoroughly. The children of the house should be encouraged to slide up and down it, for nothing polishes a floor better than a few pairs of active feet.

DUST-FREE SPECTACLES

After cleaning your spectacles, wipe them with a clean, but used, fabric-softener sheet. Dust won't stick to them.

Keeping Colours Bright

There are various ways to ensure that when you wash clothes, the colours do not fade.

☺ To stop jeans fading, soak them for half an hour in *4.5l (1gal) of water* to which *60ml (4tbsp) of distilled malt vinegar* have been added.

☺ Sometimes black clothes look faded because soap remains in the fabric. If this happens, soak the clothes in warm water and add a small amount of distilled malt vinegar or some water softener.

☺ Don't wash coloured clothes at a higher temperature than the care label suggests. If clothes are very dirty, use a washing powder created for colours that can clean at low temperatures.

☺ Soak new clothes in a bucket of cold water with a handful of salt added to it. This will help them keep their colour when you wash them for the first time.

☺ If you need to re-dye clothes such as jeans, you can do so using your washing machine. Follow the machine dye wash instructions carefully, and make sure you put your machine through a short wash cycle afterwards to remove any traces of dye.

Cleaning the Iron

For ordinary irons: clean the base using a small dab of toothpaste on a soft cloth. If this does not shift marks, rub the base of the iron gently with steel wool.
For irons with non-stick plates: using a soft cloth, clean with detergent and water or with methylated spirit.

Carpet on Ice

When you move your furniture around, you may find indentation marks in the carpet. To remove these, put an ice cube on each mark. Leave for ten hours or so and then brush up the carpet with a fork.

CLUTTER BUSTING

Do

- Clear out lofts, garages, cellars, cupboards, etc. every two or three months.

- Clear away as much as possible. If you haven't used something for years, you are unlikely to need it again.

- Take your old clothes to charity shops. In many cases, they can be used again.

- Use computer auction sites to advertise and sell unwanted items.

- Throw away items that are broken, such as old toys or kitchen crockery.

- Keep track of where you keep everything. If you don't know where an item is, it is of no use to you.

- Accept that you can't keep everything you want to.

- If you haven't used, missed or thought about an item for over a year, get rid of it.

- Clear out children's cast offs. In good condition, they are very useful to charity shops.

Don't

- Don't let clutter build up, so that you have to do a massive annual blitz.

- Don't keep items that you never use, thinking they 'might come in handy one day'.

- Don't keep lots of old clothes because they might come back into fashion. They won't.

- Don't be tempted to start buying more things on computer auction sites.

- Don't hang onto worthless items that you intend to mend in the future.

- Don't store things jumbled together in unmarked boxes. You will never be able to find them again.

- Don't hang back. If in doubt, throw it out!

- Don't forget that you cannot keep a house tidy if there are too many unused items in it.

- Don't hold on to children's mementos. One pair of baby's first shoes is enough.

OVEN TEMPERATURES FOR PASTRY

Temperatures vary for the type of pastry. Filled pies and tarts are usually baked at a high temperature to set the pastry, then finished at a lower temeprature. Always remember to pre-heat your oven to the required temperature, and also use a pre-heated baking sheet for anything that should have a crisp base.

Shortcrust	hot	220°C/425°F/Gas 7
	moderately hot	190°C/375°F/Gas 5
Sweet shortcrust	moderately hot	200°C/400°F/Gas 6
	moderate	180°C/350°F/Gas 4
Puff	very hot	240°C/475°F/Gas 9
	moderately hot	190°C/375°F/Gas 5
Choux	hot	220°C/425°F/Gas 7
	moderately hot	190°C/375°F/Gas 5
Hot-water crust	moderately hot	200°C/400°F/Gas 6
	moderate	160°C/325°F/Gas 3
Filo and strudel	hot	230°C/450°F/Gas 8
	moderate	180°C/350°F/Gas 4

VICTORIAN MULLED WINE

Boil the quantity you choose – *6 cloves, 1 cinnamon stick, ⅛ grated nutmeg or dash of mace* – in *150ml (¼pt) of water*. Add *600ml (1pt) of port* and *sugar* to taste. Boil it up and serve with thin slices of toast. Do not expect to get tipsy: once boiled, wine and other spirits lose their alcohol content.

Countdown to Christmas dinner

Step 1 — *Early December*
* Order your turkey.
* Try to find a butcher that stocks organic or free-range turkeys.
* Make sure your turkey is not too big to fit in your oven.
* Calculate that each person will eat about 450g (1lb) of turkey.

Step 2 — *Mid-December*
* Make mince pies and freeze them.
* Ice Christmas cake which you have made earlier.

Step 3 — *A week before Christmas*
* Write your shopping list and buy all food that can be stored easily.
* Make sure you buy plenty of ordinary household items to see you through the holiday, such as toilet paper and pet food.

Step 4 — *Five days before Christmas*
* If you have bought a frozen turkey, put it in the back of the fridge and start to defrost it. It will take about four or five days to thaw. Make sure that it doesn't drip on to any other food, especially salads and fruit.

Step 5 — *Two days before Christmas*
* Make cranberry sauce.
* For stuffings and bread sauce, lay out white bread in cubes on a baking tray to go stale.
* Wash and iron tablecloth and napkins.
* Polish cutlery; wash glasses and dishes. Check you have enough plates.
* Make your table decoration.

Step 6 — *Christmas Eve*
* Pick up fresh turkey from the butcher. To avoid queues, go early.
* Buy vegetables, cream and all last-minute supplies.
* Defrost your mince pies.
* Make brandy butter.
* Prepare your stuffings.
* Lay the table and set out a coffee tray for after the meal.

CHRISTMAS DAY

(for dinner at 2pm):

7 am
* Take your turkey and stuffings out of the fridge straight away.
* Stuff your turkey.
* Make sure your turkey and stuffings are at room temperature before they go into the oven, otherwise it will take longer to cook.
* Calculate the cooking time of your turkey and set your alarm to put it in the oven at the right time.

8.15 am
* Make the bread sauce. You can reheat it later.
* Prepare the vegetables. Parboil the potatoes.

11.30 am
* Put sausages and bacon rolls in with the turkey to cook.
* Put plates and serving dishes to warm.

12 noon
* Start to steam the Christmas pudding, unless you are reheating it in the microwave.
* Open red wine.

12.45 pm
* Put parboiled potatoes in the oven to roast.
* Prepare pans for steaming vegetables.

1.15 pm
* Take turkey out of oven, cover with foil and leave to rest.
* Make gravy and transfer to gravy boat. Keep warm.
* Steam vegetables.

1.30 pm
* When vegetables have steamed, serve on to warm plates.
* Put gravy boat and bread sauce dish on table.
* Check Christmas pudding; add water if it is boiling dry.
* Carve turkey. Put slices on a warm plate under foil.

2 pm
* Sit down to eat!
* Pull crackers and put on your party hats.

A COMPENDIUM OF HOUSEHOLD HINTS

Top Ten British Pets

Pet   Percentage of households

1	Cat	23.4
2	Dog	21.4
3	Rabbit	9.3
4	Goldfish	3.9
5	Budgerigar	3.6
6	Hamster	3.2
7	Tropical fish	2.4
8	Guinea pig	1.6
9	Canary	0.8
10	Other birds	0.4

Brighter Silver

- To make cleaning easier, always polish silver before it begins to look yellow or starts to turn black.

- Rinse each item in hot water to remove dust before polishing.

- Apply silver polish on a moist sponge while the items are still warm. Before starting to rub, cover the whole surface with polish.

- Use fresh, not old, dried out polish, and make sure you shake the bottle before using.

- Rub the polish in gently over tarnished areas.

- Wash off the polish with detergent and rinse the item.

- Dry the item with a soft cloth.

- Use silver 'dips' on fork tines, but not on other pieces, as it can make the silver look yellow.

- Store your silver in special flannel bags treated to stop tarnish. You can buy these in most jewellery shops.

CARING FOR HOUSEPLANTS

Do

🌱 Use sterile potting soil. For an environmentally friendly alternative to peat, use coir-based potting soil, made from recycled coconut shells.

🌱 Put a layer of stones or broken pots at the bottom of your plant pot. Be sure the pot has a drainage hole in the bottom.

🌱 Spray plants with water. They need extra humidity because of central heating.

🌱 Dust plants regularly and clean them with a solution of half milk and half water. Wipe shiny leaves with glycerine to clean.

🌱 Give each plant the right amount of sun and water (check the label or a houseplant book).

🌱 Group healthy plants that have the same requirements for light and temperature together.

🌱 Water regularly with water at room temperature.

🌱 Keep new plants away from others until you are sure they have no pests or diseases.

🌱 Put houseplants that have attracted white fly on their leaves outside in the fresh air for a short time. The cold air will kill the white fly.

Don't

🥀 Use ordinary garden soil. It is full of bacteria that will thrive inside the house.

🥀 Put houseplants in pots with no drainage or they will become too wet and die.

🥀 Keep central heating on in warm weather. It will dry out your houseplants.

🥀 Leave dust on your plants or they will be unable to breathe. They will also look drab and unhealthy.

🥀 Use very cold or hot water to water plants.

🥀 Leave plants unwatered for more than a few days.

🥀 Soak roots in water for too long or they will become soggy.

🥀 Put the plant where it looks nice, but will not be able to thrive (e.g. in a dark corner).

🥀 Move houseplants that seem to be flourishing in a particular spot. They may not thrive so well elsewhere.

🥀 Put houseplants in positions where the sun is too fierce, unless 'full sun' is specified on the label.

🥀 Leave houseplants on window sills on cold winter nights.

FLOWER ARRANGING

To make an arrangement in a vase that is too deep
- Crumple up newspaper in the bottom of the vase until the flowers come up to the right level; alternatively, stick each flower stem into a drinking straw.
- Arrange as usual in the vase. Make sure that the straws; if using, are well below the water level.

To make flower arranging easier
- Use a vase with straight sides and narrow neck.
- Arrange the flowers on the worktop, then put them into the vase in a bunch.
- Use sponge and wire (available from florists, garden centres and general household shops) to hold flowers in position.

To revive wilted flowers
- Cut a small amount off the ends of the stems, and stand them in boiling water for a few seconds.
- Then put the flowers in a vase of cold water for a further two or more hours.
- Submerge as much of the stem as possible in the cold water.

To make flowers last longer
- Cut off the bottoms of stems at an angle before you arrange them.
- Crush thick woody stems; this helps them to absorb water.
- Pull off lower leaves; this keeps the water clear and slows decay.
- Add a couple of crushed aspirins to the water; this helps your flowers stay fresher for longer.

WET WELLIES
If the insides of Wellington boots have become wet, you can dry them out quickly with a hair dryer, set at a low setting.

How to Make a Long Island Iced Tea Cocktail
Put *6 ice cubes* into a tall glass, mix together equal measures of *gin, vodka, white rum, tequila, Cointreau* and *lemon juice* with *5ml (1 tsp) of sugar*. Pour over ice and top up with cola.

Tidy Toenails
The correct way to cut toenails is to trim them straight across. Never cut the sides down to the quick. Tidy the cuticles with an orange stick with a little cotton wool wrapped around it, dipped in moisturising lotion or cuticle cream. Take care not to push the cuticles back too hard, or infections can occur.

To Stop Sweets Sticking Together
A little icing sugar sprinkled on boiled or other sticky sweets will stop them sticking together. Put the sweets in an airtight tin with the sugar and shake well.

To Patch Clothes
1. Place the patch on the wrong side of the garment and hem it all the way round.
2. Turn the fabric right side up and make slits from the centre of the hole to each corner. Then trim the ragged edge.
3. Slit each corner to within 1.25cm (½in) of the edge.
4. Turn the edges under and hem all the way round.

To Clean a Dirty Drain Grating
Gratings over outside drains can become smelly and dirty. To clean them make a coal or wood fire outdoors, then pick up the grating with a poker and put it in the fire. The fire burns away the slime and odours. Allow the grating to cool before putting it back on the drain.

A Substitute for Perfume
Dab a little vanilla extract behind your ears.

A COMPENDIUM OF HOUSEHOLD HINTS

FENG SHUI TIPS FOR THE HOME

In the hall
- Keep the main doorway clear to allow 'chi' (energy) to enter freely. Do not leave shoes outside (e.g. in the porch) as chi, which comes in with the wind, will pick up their bad odours and cause illness.
- A small indoor fountain in a central place will attract good luck.

In the bedroom
- Do not have a TV set in your bedroom. If you must, cover it with a plastic tablecloth. An ordinary tablecloth will not work!
- To sleep soundly, ensure that a solid wall is at the head of your bed.
- Do not have a mirror opposite or to one side of your bed. They can attract another person to the bed and may cause affairs.
- Do not sleep on mattresses on the floor or store anything under the bed. Chi needs to circulate under the bed to ensure health.
- Open your bedroom windows wide for at least 20 minutes a day.

In the children's rooms
- Bunk beds deprive the child on the lower bunk of fresh chi and can cause ill health. A wind chime with six metal rods may help.
- Children should write with a solid wall behind their back, to help them keep still and concentrate.

In the living room
- Do not use red chairs or sofas. The colour red represents fire. Red seating will give rise to work and money troubles.

In the kitchen
- Do not have your cooker opposite your sink. If you do, fire and water elements will clash, causing arguments in the home.
- Do not use marble tabletops in your home. They can bring work pressure. For a more relaxing life, wooden tables are best.

BEEF TEA FOR INVALIDS
- To make a nutritious beef tea, take *450g (1lb) of solid beef* (diced very small), *30g (1oz) of butter*, *one clove*, *two small onions* and *some salt*.
- Stir the meat around over heat until it produces a thin gravy; add the rest of the ingredients and then top up with *1.2l (2pt) of water*.
- Let this simmer gently for half an hour to three-quarters of an hour, skimming off every particle of fat.
- When the meat is cooked, strain the liquid through a sieve and leave to cool.
- To make plain beef tea omit the vegetables, salt and clove; the butter is taken out during the skimming.

WASHING HAIRBRUSHES
When washing a hairbrush, don't immerse the whole brush in water, as this tends to loosen the tufts.

GRACE AND DEPORTMENT
- Stand tall: the shoulders well back and the head erect.
- Always sit up straight, never lounge.
- Never fumble with the hands; keep them well to the sides.

DON'T BE 'DOWN AT HEEL'
If your shoes begin to wear down at the heels, have them repaired immediately. Badly worn shoes will ruin your entire appearance and make you appear slovenly.

MAKE HOUSEWORK GO SWIMMINGLY
Many housewives worry (with good reason) that their hair will take on the disagreeable smell of the various cleaning products that they use around the house. These ladies need worry no more. Wearing an old rubber bathing cap while cleaning will prevent any such odours from tainting the hair.

WEDDING INVITATIONS

Send invitations out well in advance. The wording of the invitation should be as follows:

> *Mr and Mrs A request the pleasure*
> *of the company of*
>
> *Mr and Mrs B*
>
> *at the marriage of their daughter*
>
> *C with Mr D E,*
>
> *on (day), (date)   at*
>
> *place*
>
> *and afterwards at (address)*
>
> *R.S.V.P*

When replying, write in the third person.
To accept, write:

> *Mr and Mrs B thank Mr and Mrs A for their kind invitation and have much pleasure in accepting.*

To refuse, write:

> *Mr and Mrs B thank Mr and Mrs A for their kind invitation and regret that they will be unable to attend, owing to a previous engagement.*

If you know your hosts well, it is polite to write a letter with the formal refusal, explaining in more detail why you cannot attend.

VIRTUES OF THE MISTRESS OF THE HOUSE

Mrs Beeton advises that, in order for the household to run properly, the mistress of the house should pursue the following virtues:

- ability to choose servants well
- careful account-keeping
- careful choice of acquaintances
- charity and benevolence
- cleanliness
- early rising
- an eye for a bargain
- frugality and economy
- good dress sense
- good temper
- hospitality

GREEN CLEANING

Today, we can buy all sorts of specialised cleaning products. However, many of them are full of strong, harmful chemicals that damage the environment. Try using some of these old-fashioned household stand-bys instead:

- ***Bicarbonate of soda:*** dozens of uses, from removing pet odours to bleaching perspiration stains and cleaning burnt pans.
- ***Distilled malt vinegar:*** use neat to remove scum marks on baths and sinks; and diluted as a hair rinse, a fabric softener, to clean windows, neutralise smells or destroy mildew.
- ***Glycerine:*** can be used to remove difficult stains such as tar, mustard, fruit juice and tomato ketchup.
- ***Lemon juice:*** a natural bleaching and disinfecting agent. It will remove rust marks and fruit juice stains from clothes, and also acts as a mild bleach.
- ***Salt:*** useful as an abrasive cleaning product (e.g. to clean off marks on baths or sinks).

A COMPENDIUM OF HOUSEHOLD HINTS

ROMAN NUMERALS

I	=	1	VIII	=	8	XV	=	15	LXXX = 80
II	=	2	IX	=	9	XX	=	20	XC = 90
III	=	3	X	=	10	XXX	=	30	C = 100
IV	=	4	XI	=	11	XL	=	40	D = 500
V	=	5	XII	=	12	L	=	50	M = 1,000
VI	=	6	XIII	=	13	LX	=	60	MM = 2,000
VII	=	7	XIV	=	14	LXX	=	70	

WRITING TO THE QUEEN

If you need to write to the Queen, begin your letter with: 'Madam'. The letter should end with the phrase: 'I have the honour to remain your Majesty's most faithful subject'.

SQUIRRELS, RATS AND MICE: KEEP OUT!

Animals can damage your property if they get into your house. The most common entry points are the roof, the eaves and dryer vents. To keep them out, cut back branches and tree limbs that they could use to jump on to your roof. Then walk around and look for other ways they could get in such as dryer vents, heating vents, chimneys and entry points for pipes and wiring. Put mesh screens over vents and chimneys. Fill any gaps around pipe entries and exit holes with steel wool, pushing it in firmly. Although rats and mice can chew through almost anything, this should stop them! Then fill the hole with foam sealant.

BATTERY SIZES AND TYPES

Type	Diameter	Height	Width	Voltage
AAA	1.05cm/²⁄₅in	4.45cm/1⁴⁄₅in	n/a	1.5V
AA	1.45cm/³⁄₅in	5cm/2in	n/a	1.5V
C	2.62cm/1in	5cm/2in	n/a	1.5V
D	3.42cm/1³⁄₁₀in	6.12cm/2²⁄₅in	n/a	1.5V
9V	n/a	4.85cm/1⁹⁄₁₀in	3.56cm/1²⁄₅in	9V

To the Rescue in the Kitchen

♦ Lumpy gravy can often be made smooth by boiling it very fiercely in the pan while stirring. If the lumps still remain, pour the gravy through a sieve before you serve it. Other kinds of sauces can also be sieved at the last minute to get rid of lumps. Use the back of the spoon to press out the juices.

♦ If you need to thicken a tomato or meat sauce, heat it quite fast to reduce it, stirring frequently so that it does not stick and burn. Rapid heating helps to dry out the sauce, since much of the water escapes as steam. Reducing a sauce in this way can help to improve the flavour of the sauce.

♦ A sauce can be thickened by adding a little flour. Mix the flour with cold water first to form a liquid. This will help to prevent lumps forming in the sauce. Then add the smooth flour and water paste to the sauce. Don't add too much flour to a sauce or it will taste dull.

♦ To stop a skin forming on thick sauces, such as cheese sauce, pour a layer of melted butter over the sauce. You can stir in the butter just before you eat it.

♦ To soak up grease in a sauce, add *5–10ml (1–2tsp) of bicarbonate of soda*, which will absorb the fat.

♦ To rescue a cake that has burnt on top, cut the burnt part off and turn it upside down. Ice the flat base and it will look and taste fine.

♦ Improve overcooked rice by rinsing it first in cold water and then heating it up in a moderate oven, spread out on a flat tray or baking dish, for half an hour. This will help to dry out and separate the grains. Check often to make sure it does not get dry and crunchy.

♦ To prevent sticky rice, rinse the grains in fresh cold water several times before cooking, leaving them to soak for a little while between each rinse. You will find this also reduces the cooking time.

Nettle Stings

You can relieve the sting of a nettle by rubbing the affected area with dock, rosemary, sage or mint leaves.

WEATHER THAT'S FOR THE BIRDS

Winter Weather

There's an old country rhyme that predicts a mild wet winter.

If there's ice at Martinmas will bear a duck,
There'll be nothing after but sludge and muck.

Martinmas falls on 11 November.

Storms Ahead

When gulls appear in the fields, expect a storm.

Sea-gull, sea-gull sit on the sand;
It's never good weather when they're on the land.

Rain Prediction

If the cock goes crowing to bed,
He'll certainly rise with a watery head.

In other words, it will be raining next morning.

In many countries, a green woodpecker's loud laughing call is a portent of rain.

Calm Before The Storm

When swallows fly high in search of insects, it is taken as a sign of a brief period of fine weather followed by a thunderstorm. This may be because the warm air currents that carry the flies aloft are frequently a prelude to a storm.

CLEANING JEWELLERY

Gem	Method
Diamonds	Add a few drops of ammonia and two drops of dishwashing liquid to a bowl of hot water. Put your diamond ring(s) into a tea strainer and dip into the mixture briefly. Rinse in bowl of cold water.
Emeralds	Very soft, will absorb water and may crack. Clean professionally.
Gold	Wash in a bowl of soapy water. Rub gently with a soft toothbrush to get dirt out of details and links.
Jade	Wash in soapy water. Dry with a soft cloth.
Opals	Do not wash – it's porous.
Pearls	Buff gently with a soft cloth dipped in olive oil.
Rubies	As for diamonds
Sapphires	As for diamonds
Silver	Make a paste of lemon juice and bicarbonate of soda. Rub in with a soft toothbrush, let dry; then brush off with a soft, dry toothbrush. Polish with a soft cloth
Turquoise	As for opals

WASHING DELICATES

Put delicate items such as tights and scarves into a pillowcase before washing them. This will stop them getting tangled and possibly torn by the machine's spin cycle.

SHORT LEGS

If you have a table that wobbles because one of the legs is shorter than the others, cut a piece of cork so that it fits underneath and raises the short leg to the right level. When you have got the right level, stick the piece of cork to the table leg with wood glue.

HOW TO STOP GEMS FROM DROPPING OUT

Have a jeweller check that the prongs are not loose occasionally.

A COMPENDIUM OF HOUSEHOLD HINTS

What's in Season This Month?

Although you can buy almost any type of fruit and vegetable in the supermarkets, at any time of year, locally produced fruit and vegetables in season often taste better and cost less. Below is a seasonal guide to British vegetables and fruit:

JANUARY/FEBRUARY
    broccoli, Brussels sprouts, cabbages, kale, leeks, parsnips, potatoes (old), swedes
    apples

MARCH/APRIL
    beetroot, Brussels sprouts, spring greens, sprouting broccoli, Swiss chard, turnips
    apples, rhubarb

MAY/JUNE
    asparagus, cabbages, lettuce, radishes, shallots, spring onions, spinach, turnips, watercress
    cherries, rhubarb, strawberries

JULY/AUGUST
    broad beans, dwarf and runner beans, carrots, cauliflowers, courgettes, lettuces, marrows, onions, peas, potatoes (new), radishes, tomatoes
    blackcurrants, cherries, gooseberries, peaches, raspberries, redcurrants, strawberries

SEPTEMBER/OCTOBER
    carrots, cucumber, lettuce, onions, potatoes (old), pumpkins, runner beans, swedes, sweetcorn, tomatoes
    apples, blackberries, pears, plums

NOVEMBER/DECEMBER
    Brussels sprouts, cabbages, cauliflowers, celery, leeks, parsnips, potatoes (old), swedes
    apples

TO WHITEN COTTON SOCKS

Soak socks for an hour in *4.5l (1gal) of hot water* and *2tbsp of dishwasher detergent*. Afterwards, wash them as usual in the washing machine. For an ecological alternative, boil the socks in a saucepan with some slices of lemon. Again, wash them as normal afterwards.

CLEANING LAMPSHADES

Clean lampshades carefully, or they may end up looking dirtier than before, with streaks of dirt where you have wiped them, which are of course illuminated by the lightbulb.

- Fabric lampshades – A vacuum cleaner with a brush attachment
- Glass or plastic shades – Clean with a damp cloth
- Paper shades – A plain duster or whisk broom
- Silk shades – Professionally clean

HANGING CURTAINS

Flimsy curtains can be made to hang straight by tucking coins into the hems. The coins should be placed at regular intervals, and then stitched into place.

Short curtains can be lengthened by moving the hooks at the top first. If this isn't enough, try changing the type of rail: curtain rods with hoops often add extra inches. Alternatively, sew a contrasting band of fabric to the hem; choose a fabric of the same weight as the curtains.

When you measure up for curtains, a rule of thumb is that your curtain fabric needs to be twice the width of your window, to allow for the right amount of gathering. To economise, use one and a half times the amount of fabric, but don't make it any less or your curtains will look too flat when drawn.

REMOVING EGG STAINS ON SILVER

Eggs can turn silver black; to remove the black stain, rub the spoon or other article with a little salt between your finger and thumb.

A COMPENDIUM OF HOUSEHOLD HINTS

ROASTING TIMES AND TEMPERATURES FOR GAME

There are three ways to cook game. Some game like boar can only be slow-roasted, otherwise it will be tough.

	Fast-roasting (230°C/450°F/ Gas 8 for total roasting time)	*Combined High and Low Heat* (Sear at 240°C/475°F/ Gas 9 for 10 min, then reduce the heat to 180°C/350°F/Gas 4)	*Slow-roasting* (150°C/300°F/ Gas 2 for total time)
Grouse	20–30 min	n/a	n/a
Hare	30–40 min	n/a	n/a
Partridge	20–25 min	n/a	n/a
Pheasant	30–45 min	n/a	n/a
Pigeon	20–30 min	n/a	n/a
Rabbit	30 min	n/a	n/a
Snipe	10–15 min	n/a	n/a
Venison:		*(rare)*	
Saddle	n/a	8–9 min per 450g (1lb)	n/a
Haunch	n/a	9–10 min per 450g (1lb)	n/a
Wild boar	n/a	n/a	35–40 min per 450g (1lb)
Wild duck	20–30 min	n/a	n/a
Woodcock	15–20 min	n/a	n/a

LITRES TO GALLONS

Gallons x 4.55 = number of litres; litres x 0.22 = number of gallons.

Gallons	1	2	3	4	5	6	7	8	9	10
Litres	4.55	9.1	13.65	18.2	22.75	27.3	31.85	36.4	40.95	45.5

Litres	1	2	3	4	5	6	7	8	9	10
Gallons	0.22	0.44	0.66	0.88	1.10	1.32	1.54	1.76	1.98	2.20

COCKTAIL GLASSES

Serving cocktails in the appropriate glasses helps add style and sophistication to any drinks party.

Cocktail glass
For martinis and other cocktails, this is the classic, triangular-shaped glass often associated with sophisticated drinking.

Collins
Holds about the same amount as the highball, but is slimmer and taller. Used for spirits mixed with other drinks, especially fizzy drinks and frosted drinks.

Highball
Taller than the old-fashioned tumbler. Used for spirits that are mixed with other drinks, such as gin and tonic, scotch and soda, and so on.

Liqueur, sherry and port glasses
Small glasses for drinking fortified wines. They come in a wide variety of shapes, with a capacity from under *30* to *150ml (1–5fl oz)*. Liqueur glasses are generally smaller than sherry and port glasses.

Old-fashioned
A short, squat glass known as a 'lowball' or 'rocks' glass. Used for serving drinks with ice.

Pony
A pony is a glass with a stem which holds *30ml (1fl oz)* shots of spirits.

Shot
Used to measure *45ml (½fl oz)* shot of spirits.

Tumbler
A large glass that is wider at the top than the bottom. Often used for soft drinks and for water, as well as for spirits mixed with other drinks.

Cigar Types

Churchill
17.5cm (7in) by 47-ring gauge (i.e. diameter of a cigar). Named after Winston Churchill.

Corona
15cm (6in) by 42-ring gauge. The standard cigar – the corona has an open end (or 'foot', the end that is lit) and a closed, usually rounded head (smoking end).

Culebra
Three panatellas plaited to form one cigar.

Diadema
A large cigar of 20cm (8in) or longer by 52-ring gauge, with open foot.

Panatella
17.5cm (7in) by 38-ring gauge. Usually longer and thinner than coronas. With a pointed, closed head.

Perfecto
A closed pointed head, closed foot and a bulge in the middle.

Robusto
12.5cm (5in) by 50-ring gauge.

Torpedo
Similar to the perfecto, except that it is not as round. It is rolled so that it is smaller at each end, with a bulge in the middle.

Periods of British Antique Furniture

Name	Period
Elizabethan/Tudor	mid-1500s–early 1600s
Jacobean	early 1600s–late 1600s
Queen Anne	early 1700s–mid-1700s
Chippendale	mid-1700s
Adam Bros	late 1700s
Hepplewhite	late 1700s
Sheraton	late 1700s

SEWING STITCHES

BACKSTITCH

Used to make a strong seam that will not tear easily when subjected to pressure. Take one stitch forward and lock it by stitching another shorter one on top. For a perfect backstitch, there should be no gaps between the stitches.

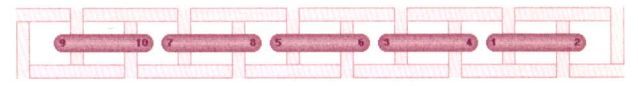

BLANKET STITCH

Used to 'whip' fabric that may fray (e.g. the edge of a blanket). It also has an ornamental value, and is sometimes used in a contrasting colour to the fabric. Button holes, stitched in lighter weight thread, are the same basic stitch as blanket stitch and have the same use: to prevent fraying.

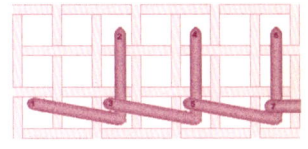

CROSS STITCH

Used for hemming raw edges liable to fray (e.g. trouser hems).

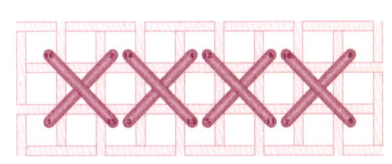

RUNNING STITCH

A series of small, neat stitches running forward, with gaps in between. It is used as a rough, temporary seam or, when the thread is pulled tight, as a way of gathering fabric. It is not useful as a proper stitch to make strong seams, as the fabric is not closed all the way along the seam, and it is easily broken.

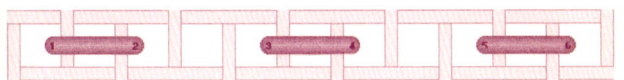

A COMPENDIUM OF HOUSEHOLD HINTS

Most Popular Dog Breeds in UK

1. Labrador
2. German Shepherd
3. West Highland White Terrier
4. Golden Retriever
5. Cocker Spaniel
6. Springer Spaniel
7. Cavalier King Charles Spaniel
8. Boxer
9. Yorkshire Terrier
10. Staffordshire Bull Terrier

Untangling a Necklace

To untangle a fine chain or necklace, put it on a sheet of greaseproof paper. Add a drop or two or plain massage oil or baby oil. Take a couple of needles and work to untangle the knot.

To prevent the problem from happening again, hang necklaces from small hooks by your dressing table or inside a wardrobe door. They will look decorative and you will be able to choose each easily.

Vinegar in the Kitchen

Vinegar is a useful ingredient to have on hand and will help sort out any number of culinary problems.

- If a dish is too sweet, add a spoonful of cider vinegar.
- Rub a spoonful or two into meat, to marinate or tenderise it.
- Add a large spoonful to the water when you are poaching eggs – they will keep their shape better.
- Add a little to the water when you are cooking artichokes or red-coloured vegetables such as red cabbage or beets. The vinegar will help them keep their colour.
- If you've reduced the salt in a recipe, add a few drops of vinegar, and you won't notice the missing salt so much.

To Make Perfect Coffee in a Cafetière

- Boil a kettle using fresh, cold water.
- Take the kettle off the heat as soon as it it boiled.
- Warm the cafetière by adding a small amount of hot water and swishing it around. Then tip it out.
- Put a spoonful of coffee per person into the cafetière.
- Allow the water to come just off the boil before pouring it over the coffee so that it doesn't scorch the coffee and stop it from releasing its full aroma.
- Leave the coffee to stand for several minutes before pushing down the plunger in the cafetière.
- Pour and enjoy, adding cream or milk and sugar to taste.

Butterscotch Sundae

Heat *60ml (4tbsp) of butter* and *120ml (4fl oz) of double cream* in a small saucepan over a medium heat. Once the butter is melted, stir in *85g (3oz) of brown sugar*. Continue to cook the mixture over a gentle heat for about ten minutes until the sauce thickens and become smooth and glossy. Serve the sauce warm over vanilla ice cream. Finish with a garnish of whipped cream and a maraschino cherry.

Speed Conversion

To convert kilometres per hour (km/h) to miles per hour (mph), multiply by 1.609. To convert miles per hour (mph) to kilometres per hour (km/h), multiply by 0.621.

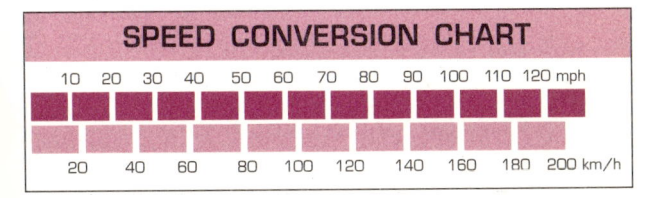

SPEED CONVERSION CHART

10	20	30	40	50	60	70	80	90	100	110	120 mph
20	40	60	80	100	120	140	160	180	200 km/h		

Addressing Persons of Nobility and Rank

When writing or speaking to persons of nobility and rank, remember the following:

The Queen should be addressed as 'Your Majesty'. When writing to the Queen, address her as 'Madam'.

Dukes are the top members of the aristocracy. They should be addressed as 'Duke' by social equals; servants should call them 'Your Grace'.

Marquises are the eldest sons of dukes. Call them 'Marquis' if you consider yourself a social equal, or 'My Lord' if you don't.

Viscounts, Earls and ***Barons*** are all known as 'My Lord'.

Baronets are addressed as Sir (Christian Name) (Surname). When writing to them, if their title is not hereditary but gained in the House of Lords, 'Bart' can be added to the end of the name. A baronet's wife is addressed as Lady (Surname). Thus, Sir James Burney's wife will be known as Lady Burney.

Knights are those who hold the honour of 'Knight Commander of the Victorian Order'. They are also addressed as Sir (Christian Name) (Surname). Their wives are formally known as Lady (Surname), but many people now address knights' wives by their Christian names. Thus, the wife of Sir Jeremy Harwood may be called Lady Sarah instead of the correct Lady Harwood.

Bishops The archbishops of Canterbury and York are called 'Your Grace'. Bishops are addressed as 'Bishop' by friends and equals, or sometimes nowadays as Bishop (Christian Name): 'Bishop John'. Those of lower standing are expected to call the bishop 'My Lord'.

The Lord Mayor should be addressed as 'Your Worship'.

ADDRESSING ORDINARY PEOPLE

THE CLERGY

Clergymen are sometimes referred to by the old-fashioned term of 'parsons'.

Canon   A canon is a high-ranking vicar, and can be addressed as 'Canon (Surname)'.

Minister   Usually refers to a non-conformist clergyman who, as part of his or her religious beliefs, does not accept a formal title.

Monk   Referred to as 'Brother (first name)'. The exception is the head of a monastery, or Father Superior, who is addressed as 'Father (first name)'.

Nun   Addressed as 'Sister (first name)'. The exception is the head of the convent, or Mother Superior, who is called 'Mother (first name)'.

Priest   In the Roman Catholic and High Anglican church, priests are referred to as 'Father'.

Rector   A vicar or rector is traditionally a person who has 'a living', that is, who is in charge of a parish. He or she can be called 'Vicar', 'Rector' or 'Mr/Mrs/Ms (Surname)'. When writing to a rector, address him or her as 'The Rev.' (Christian Name) (Surname).

Vicar   *See* Rector.

THE MEDICAL PROFESSION

Doctor   Shortened to Dr, it is used to note general practitioners (GPs) and some other health professionals.

Surgeon   Known as 'Mr' or 'Mrs', never Doctor.

OTHERS

Esquire   Shortened to Esq., this was used to address all other ranks of society other than the aristocracy. Fallen into disuse and is considered archaic.

Mr   The traditional title to use when writing to tradesmen.

A COMPENDIUM OF HOUSEHOLD HINTS

ROASTING TIMES AND TEMPERATURES FOR BEEF

Beef is roasted in different ways depending on the cut. The best roasting joints are tender. They come from young animals and from parts of the animal that do the least work such as the back and hind legs. After roasting be sure to rest the joint – it will be juicier and easier to carve.

	Fast-roasting	*Combined High and Low Heat*	*Slow-roasting*
BEEF	(240°C/475°F/ Gas 9 for total roasting time)	(Sear at 240°C/475°F/ Gas 9 for 15 min, then reduce the heat to 180°C/350°F/Gas 4)	(150°C/300°F/ Gas 2 for total time)
Fillet	*Rare* 7 min per 450g (1lb) *Medium* 10 min per 450g (1lb)	n/a	n/a
Prime rib*	n/a	*Rare* 8–10 min per 450g (1lb) [10–12 min] *Medium* 10–12 min per 450g (1lb) [12–15 min] *Well-done* 15–18 min per 450g (1lb) [18–20 min]	n/a
Wing rib*	n/a		n/a
Sirloin*	n/a		n/a
Rump*	n/a		n/a
Fore rib*	n/a		n/a
Aitchbone cut*	n/a	n/a	
Back rib*	n/a	n/a	*Medium* 20–25 min per 450g (1lb) *Well-done* 30–35 min per 450g (1lb)
Thick rib*	n/a	n/a	
Topside*	n/a	n/a	
Silverside*	n/a	n/a	
Top rump*	n/a	n/a	

On the bone and boneless. Times specifically for boneless joints in square brackets.

TO DRY HERBS

Pull off each leaf separately and spread out in a single layer in a tin tray. Bake in a medium oven until the leaves are dry enough to rub into powder. Leave to cool. Then crush. Store in wide-mouthed bottles, which should be corked tightly.

MAKE YOUR OWN FURNITURE POLISH

Grate *55g (2oz) of natural beeswax* (if the beeswax is too hard, warm it for a couple of seconds on the lowest setting of a microwave). Put the beeswax in a jar with a lid and add *150ml (5fl oz) of pure turpentine*. Place the lid on the jar, but do not screw it tight. Stand the jar in a dish or bowl of hot (but not boiling) water. This will melt the beeswax to form a paste. Screw the lid down tightly and shake the jar well to mix the beeswax with the turpentine. Leave to cool completely before using.

EASY CLEANUP FOR PAINTERS AND DECORATORS

- To keep the paint kettle clean, line it with silver foil. Throw away the foil after you have finished.
- To keep your roller tray paint-free, place it inside a plastic bag. The bag should be loose so that you can fill the depression in the tray with paint. Tie at the top end. Smooth the bag into the depression; pour in paint. When you are done, untie, turn inside out and discard bag. All the paint will be on the bag, not in the tray.

PAMPER YOUR TOMATO PLANTS

Cut down on watering tomatoes by lining the hole you plant them in with a (clean) disposable nappy. Dig a hole 15–23cm (6–9in) deep, line with a nappy, plastic side down, and cover with a layer of soil. Then plant your tomato seedling as usual. The nappy holds in water, so you will need to water less often.

A COMPENDIUM OF HOUSEHOLD HINTS

CHRISTENINGS

- ✝ The baby should wear white; if a family christening robe is available, it is a lovely touch.
- ✝ Originally, babies were christened at ordinary Sunday services, especially on Easter Sunday; today, special services are often held in which children are christened.
- ✝ The christening symbolises that the church is receiving a new member.
- ✝ A baby boy has two male godparents and one female; a baby girl has two female godparents and one male.
- ✝ The godparents traditionally give the child a present made of silver.
- ✝ Godparents are expected to remember the child's birthday, and to take responsibility for the religious and moral guidance throughout his or her life.
- ✝ According to ancient superstition, the baby should cry when being baptised; otherwise it is thought that the devil has not come out of it.

DRIED FLOWERS

Tie a small bunch of flowers with string. Hang it upside down in a dry, dark, cool place indoors. After a few days, the flowers will have dried out. Experiment with different species – some flowers dry out better than others. Bud roses, cornflowers and large daisies are excellent.

TO CLEAN PAINT BRUSHES

- ♦ Water-based emulsion paint can be cleaned off brushes easily with washing up liquid or laundry detergent and warm water.
- ♦ Rollers should be rolled over newspaper to remove as much paint as possible, and then washed with washing up liquid or laundry detergent and warm water.
- ♦ For oil-based paints such as gloss, wipe as much paint as you can off the brushes with newspaper; then swish the brushes in white spirit. Finally, wash them in soapy water and rinse them.
- ♦ Repeat until clean.

How to Make Perfect Pastry

DO

✔ Work on a cold surface in the kitchen.

✔ Make sure your hands are cool; otherwise, the pastry will warm up.

✔ Chill the pastry for an hour or so in the fridge before you roll it out.

✔ Flour the work surface and the rolling pin before you roll out the dough.

✔ Use a cold rolling pin, or a bottle of iced water, to roll out the dough.

✔ Put a glass pastry dish on a metal baking tray in the oven to disperse heat evenly.

✔ Brush the pastry with egg white before adding the filling to keep the pastry from getting soggy.

DON'T

✘ Don't try to make pastry on a hot surface in a steamy kitchen.

✘ Don't have sweaty hands – run them under a cold tap and dry them before you start work.

✘ Don't roll out warm pastry. It will stick to the work surface.

✘ Don't put flour directly on to the dough; it will only make it sticky.

✘ Don't let the rolling pin heat up as you roll out the dough.

✘ Don't put a glass dish straight onto the rack, as it won't get hot enough.

✘ Don't let the middle of a pastry case become soggy.

A COMPENDIUM OF HOUSEHOLD HINTS

How to Play Hunt the Slipper

Players, who should number quite a few (from six people minimum up to about twenty maximum), sit in a circle close together. In the centre of the circle is the person chosen to 'chase the slipper'. The people in the circle hold their hands behind their backs, with one of them holding a slipper. The slipper is passed around from hand to hand, and occasionally a player will tap the slipper on the floor in front of his or her feet. The hunter turns about, trying to find the source of the sound, until he or she finally catches the player tapping the slipper.

Paper Sizes

Size	Millimetres	Inches
A1	594 x 841	23⅜ x 33⅛
A2	420 x 594	16½ x 23⅜
A3	297 x 420	11¾ x 16½
A4	210 x 297	8¼ x 11¾
A5	148 x 210	5⅞ x 8¼
A6	105 x 148	4⅛ x 7⅞
	Envelopes	
DL (⅓ A4)	110 x 220	4½ x 8½
C5 (½ A4)	229 x 162	9 x 6½
C4L (full A4)	324 x 229	12½ x 9

To Clean Paint off Hands

White spirit cleans paint off hands, but it can irritate and dry out the skin. As an alternative, rub a small amount of vegetable oil into your hands to remove paint. Afterwards, dry your hands on a paper towel. Then wash with soap and water as usual.

To Clean Baths

When a scum forms on the inside of a bath, rub the area with dry salt, and the scum will come off easily.

LAYING A FIRE

1 Rake out cinders and ashes from the grate and remove them. Check that they are completely cold before throwing them away.

2 Leave some cinders in the fireplace, crumple up some pieces of newspaper, or roll them diagonally into long straws. Then simply place these in the grate.

3 Lay some fine kindling on top of the newspaper.

4 On top of this, place some large pieces of wood.

5 Small pieces of coal can go on top of the larger pieces of wood. Arrange some at the back as well as in the middle of the grate, but do not put them too far forward, or the fire will smoke.

6 Open the dampers under the grate to let the right amount of draught in under the fire. If the grate is open, arrange more wood and coal on top for a bigger fire.

7 If kindling is damp, or if you need to light a fire quickly, use fire lighters under the coal or larger pieces of wood. Make sure to store your fire lighters in a place well away from the fire, to prevent untimely accidents.

8 Light the fire and use bellows, if you have them, to help it along. If it doesn't light easily, the newspaper, wood and coal may be too tightly packed in. Use a poker to create more air spaces in the fire.

9 Always use a fireguard when you leave an open fire unattended. If children are in the house, use a special safety fireguard.

10 An inexpensive, fireproof hearth rug laid in front of the fire is a good way of preventing coal and sparks from burning holes in the carpet if they jump out of the fireplace.

A COMPENDIUM OF HOUSEHOLD HINTS

How to Pass the Port

- Only white port is drunk as an aperitif. All other kinds of port are for after-dinner drinking.

- Store port at 13–18°C (55–65°F) horizontally, at 65 per cent humidity. If there is a white mark painted on the side of the bottle, keep this side facing up.

- Port should be served at 18–20°C (65–68°F).

- Use a proper port glass, which is like an elongated wine goblet.

- Only half fill the glass, so you can savour the aroma in the glass.

- In the navy, the port was traditionally passed 'from port to port' (i.e. clockwise). The decanter of port should be placed in front of the host, who serves the guest to his right. The host then passes the decanter to his left. The guest on the left again passes the decanter to the left, until the decanter comes back round to the host, when the sequence can start again!

- One way of making sure the port is passed on, is to ask the guest closest to the decanter if he knows the Bishop of Norwich. If the guest says no, the questioner must say, 'The Bishop is a frightfully good fellow but he never passes the port!'

- Guests sometimes bet on what the vintage and shipper of the port is. Usually, only small amounts of money change hands.

- The year and the house will be branded on the cork.

- Serve port with cheese. Stilton and other blue cheeses, Cheddar and Gloucester are particularly good. Nuts and berry-flavoured desserts also go well with port.

- Do not re-cork a bottle of port. It is known as the 'wine of philosophy' – drink it all, among friends, if you can!

WALLPAPERING TERMS

Flocked wallpaper
Wallpaper with a raised pattern on the surface. Hides imperfections.

Lining paper
Plain, unfinished wallpaper. Used to create a smooth surface before painting or wallpapering.

Steam stripper
Used to remove wallpaper by loosening the glue with steam. The stripper works like a large steam iron. When it is pressed to the wall, it loosens old wallpaper, which can then be stripped off with a blade. Steamers can be bought or hired.

Textured wallpaper
Hides imperfections and is normally painted after being hung.

Vinyl wallpaper
Wallpaper with a slight sheen. Easy to wipe clean. Suitable for kitchens and bathrooms.

KEEPING BREAD FRESH

A slice of potato or apple in the bread bin will help to keep bread fresh. Bread bins should be cleaned regularly, in order to stop mould from developing.

TO PACK GLASS OR CHINA

Use soft straw or hay to pack glass or china. If they are to be sent a long way, and are heavy, the hay or straw should be a little damp, which will prevent them slipping about. The largest and heaviest things should be put at the bottom of the box or hamper. Use plenty of straw, and pack the articles tightly.

HOW TO MAKE A SCREWDRIVER COCKTAIL

Crack *4–5 ice cubes* and put into a cocktail shaker with *37.5ml (1¼fl oz) vodka* and *97.5ml (3¼fl oz) orange juice*. Shake well and pour into a highball glass.

Turkey Cooking Times

Size of turkey
(kilograms/pounds)   *Hours*
3.6–5.4kg (8–12lb)   2½ to 3
5.4–7.2kg (12–16lb)   3 to 3½
7.2–9kg (16–20lb)   3½ to 4
9–10.8kg (20–24lb)   4 to 5

These times are based on a turkey cooked in a foil tent at 170°C (325°F/Gas mark 3). Add 30 minutes for stuffed turkey.

Famous Modern Chair Designers

Designer	*Dates*
Alvar Aalto	1898–1976
Marcel Breuer	1902–81
Charles Eames	1907–78
Le Corbusier	1887–1965
Charles Rennie Mackintosh	1868–1928
Ludwig Mies van der Rohe	1886–1969

Moth Prevention without Mothballs

If you don't like the smell of mothballs, try deterring moths by using citrus fruits. Cut the peel off oranges and lemons and slice these into thin strips. Lay them out on a baking sheet to dry in a warm room. Once the peels have dried out completely, put them in with your stored clothes and they will help to deter moths. And remember, moths are attracted to dirty or stained clothes – before you store clothes away, make sure they are completely clean.

Brightening Tapestry

Upholstery and cushions made from tapestry can be cleaned by rubbing damp salt into the stitching. Leave the salt for half an hour and then brush off. The colours should be bright and clean again.

TIPS FOR WORKING WITH GLOSS PAINT
- To stop paint hardening on brushes when you are taking a break, wrap the bristles in cling film to prevent the paint from drying.
- To reduce paint odour in a room, cut an onion in half and place it on a saucer. This will absorb the smell.

HOLIDAY CARE FOR PLANTS
Put your plants in the bath when you go on holiday. Place the plants on a few old towels and add an inch or so of water.

HOW TO DECANT VINTAGE PORT
Stand the bottle upright for as long as possible before decanting, to let the sediment settle in the bottom of the bottle. Old bottles are sometimes difficult to open. If the cork breaks, strain the wine while decanting. If you are using a funnel, there is normally a wire mesh on it. If not, use a piece of muslin rather than a filter paper. Slowly pour the port into the decanter. Do this in one motion, until you reach the sediment in the bottom of the bottle. If you are using a funnel, you will see the sediment start to appear on its sides. Discard the rest of the port. Holding a candle or torch to the bottle may help you see the sediment.

THE REALLY USEFUL HERBS
Bay leaf	Dried leaves sprinkled over the garden are a natural insecticide.
Lavender	Nourishes all sorts of beneficial, nectar-feeding insects in the garden, to help pollinate your flowers. Dried sprigs of lavender also repel moths in the house.
Lemon balm	Dried, powdered leaves are a powerful insecticide in the garden.
Rue	Can help stop cats coming into your garden.
Yarrow	A great natural fertiliser. Its leaves can be added to the compost heap to speed up the process. It also repels insects.

WEDDING ETIQUETTE

Today, the way people choose to get married varies according to their beliefs, tastes and budget, but some traditions are still in common use:

- Send out wedding invitations at least six weeks before the date.
- Wedding banns are read for three consecutive Sundays in the parish church where the wedding is to take place.
- The bride's parents pay for the wedding, but the bridegroom pays for flowers for the bride and bridesmaid, the bride's mother's corsage, the bridesmaids' presents, and also fees for the vicar, the church and the ceremony.
- The bride is traditionally married in her home town symbolising the idea that the bridegroom is taking her away from her father.
- The bride's father or an older relative or friend proposes the health of the bride and bridegroom, and the bridegroom replies. He then proposes the health of the bridesmaids and pages.
- The best man replies to the bridegroom on behalf of the bridesmaids (who should be unmarried – married women can be matrons of honour).
- The bride should wear 'something old, something new, something borrowed, something blue'.
- The bride should arrive last at the ceremony, but the bridegroom must always be on time for the ceremony.
- The bride takes the arm of her father to walk up the aisle, and the bridesmaids follow. At the top of the aisle, she meets the bridegroom, waiting at the end of the pew; here, she takes his arm.
- The best man carries the ring and gives it to the bridegroom.
- The bridegroom puts the ring on the third finger of his bride's left hand when instructed to by the officiant.
- The bride should traditionally be veiled; when the parson pronounces the pair 'man and wife' she puts her veil back and the bridegroom can kiss her.
- The civil part of the service is where the bride and bridegroom sign the register in the vestry, with the parson acting as registrar.

ON HEARING THE FIRST CUCKOO

According to superstition, much depends on the direction from which you hear the cuckoo! If the call comes from your right or in front, all will be well. A call from your left or behind is unlucky.

HOW TO TIE A BOW TIE

First put the right end over and under the left end and pull tight to the neck (1). Then double over the left end of the tie to make a bow (2). Next, bring the right end of the tie down over the bow (3). The last step is to double back the right end behind the bow and pull through (4). Finally, pull the bow tight (5).

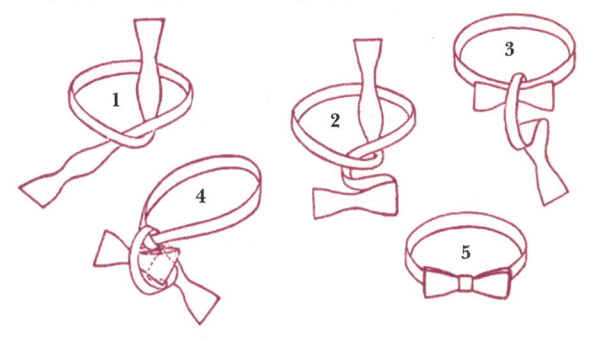

SKIN FOOD

To make a rich skin food for dry skin, mix together:

15g (½oz) cocoa butter
15g (½oz) white wax
15g (½oz) lanolin
120ml (4fl oz) almond oil
30ml (1fl oz) orange flower water

Massage a little into your face every day for a beautiful complexion. It keeps for one month and doesn't need storing in the fridge.

ESSENTIAL KITCHEN KIT

Baking dishes Various sizes.

Bottle opener

Casserole dishes Dishes with lids that you can transfer from stove top to oven are useful for stews and other slow-cooking dishes.

Chopping boards (3) One for bread, one for vegetables and one for meat.

Colander

Corkscrew

Fish slice

Food processor

Frying pans Large non-stick frying pan with a flat bottom and a small frying pan for omelettes, etc.

Grater

Kettle

Kitchen paper

Knife sharpener

Knives Various sizes, plus one serrated bread knife.

Ladle

Measuring cups

Measuring jug Marked in both metric and imperial.

Microwave

Old pan For boiling clothes, socks, etc.

Potato peeler

Roasting tins Large and small.

Saucepans with lids Three sizes: small, medium and large.

Scales

Set of British standard measuring spoons To measure 1 tbsp, 1 tsp and below and metric measures.

Sieve

Slotted spoon

Tea towels

Timer

Tin opener

Toaster Buy one that will fit wide slices of bread.

Whisk

Wok

Wooden spoons

ESSENTIAL TOOL KIT

Carpenter's claw hammer
G-Clamp
Drill bits
Electric drill
Measuring tape
Pliers
Saw, Crosscut
Screwdrivers, Common-tip
Screwdrivers, Phillips-head
Spirit level
Stanley knife
Wrench, Adjustable

GETTING RED WINE OUT OF CARPETS

Opinion is divided on how to get red wine stains out of carpets. The following methods all have their advocates, but on one point they are all united: speed is essential! You must work quickly before the stain sets and keep cleaning until no more red stains show on your cloths.

Salt
Pour salt on to the red wine – the salt soaks up the wine. Continue pouring until the surface is dry. Leave overnight. In the morning brush and vacuum up the salt. Be thorough. When all the salt is gone, use the soda water method or wash with carpet cleaner.

Soda water
Pour soda water on to the spilled red wine. Mop up with cloths or paper towels. Continue until no more red shows on your cloths.

White wine
Pour white wine on to the spilled red wine. Mop up with cloths or paper towels. Continue until no more red shows on your cloths.

A COMPENDIUM OF HOUSEHOLD HINTS

POPULAR CHINA TEAS
Chun Mee (Precious Eyebrows)
Gunpowder ... Rolled into pellets
Jasmine ... Flower scented
Keemun ... Lightly scented
Lapsang Souchong ... Smoke-dried
Lung Ching (Dragon Well)
Oolong ... 'Semi-green'
Pai Mu Tan (White Peony) ... White
Pu-erh ... Medicinal
Young Hyson ... Golden

POPULAR INDIA TEAS
Assam ... Full-bodied
Darjeeling ... Muscatel flavour
Masala ... Blended with spices
Nilgiri ... Brisk and fragrant

POPULAR BRITISH BLENDS
Earl Grey ... Bergamot-perfumed
English Breakfast ... Full aroma
Irish Breakfast ... Full-bodied
Queen Anne* ... Blended Assam
Russian Caravan ... Strong, smoky

Fortnum and Mason's famous blend

TAKING TEA WITH THE QUEEN
The Queen's garden parties are held in the summer in the gardens of Buckingham Palace or at Windsor Castle. Each garden party is held from 4–6pm, and numbers guests of up to 8,000. The menu is:

27,000 cups of tea*
20,000 glasses of fruit squash
20,000 various sandwiches
10,000 glasses of iced coffee
9,000 buttered drop scones
9,000 fruit tartlets
8,000 slices chocolate and lemon cake
5,000 bridge rolls
4,500 slices Dundee cake
4,500 slices Majorca cake
3,500 slices chocolate or jam swiss roll
3,500 vanilla or strawberry ice creams
3,000 buttercake fingers

* The tea is blended by Mason Lyons, exclusively for the Queen's garden parties. It is a blend of Darjeeling and Assam teas, with a unique flavour of peaches and muscat grapes.

POPULAR CHINA PATTERNS

Today, the most popular British china designs are plain, such as Jasper Conran's range for Wedgwood or Denby's Blue Jetty. However, in the past, classic patterns were very flowery and ornate. These are still popular and are collected by enthusiasts around the world.

Name	Description	Manufacturer
Blue Willow	Chinese design of a pair of swallows over a bridge	Royal Worcester Spode
Old Country Roses	Pink, red and gold roses	Royal Albert (Royal Doulton)
Blue Italian	Chinese border, central scene of Roman ruins	Spode
Botanic Garden	Leaf border, central floral design	Portmeirion
Jasperware (Blue)	White bas-relief figure on blue	Wedgwood
Jasperware (Sage Green)	White bas-relief figure on green	Wedgwood
Sarah's Garden*	Botanical sketches of plants, flowers and herbs	Wedgwood

Designed for Sarah, Josiah Wedgwood's wife

A COMPENDIUM OF HOUSEHOLD HINTS

Tips For a Successful Compost

With proper treatment, grass mowings, weeds, vegetable peelings and dead leaves can be used to make a rich, healthy fertiliser and soil conditioner for the garden. You can set it up in the following order:

Site Well away from house or seating areas in the garden.

Bins and boxes Make sure the base of the heap is aerated, so that matter decomposes swiftly. Put up on bricks.

From the garden Grass mowings, weeds, most kinds of plant – except large woody branches and stems and evergreen leaves and pine needles – which take a very long time to rot down.

From the kitchen Vegetable and fruit peelings, teabags and egg shells. Small amounts of newspaper or cardboard can also be added. Never put meat or animal fats on your compost heap; it attracts rats.

A good mixture Make sure you mix the different kinds of materials together thoroughly.

Moisture Keep damp, but not wet. In summer, water the heap. In winter, protect it from too much rain with an old carpet.

Warmth Maintain the right temperature at the centre of your compost heap – which helps to kill weeds and sterilise the material – by keeping it warm. In cold weather, place an old carpet on top of the heap.

Activators Add animal manure, bone, fish meal and seaweed products. A layer of lime helps to neutralise acid soils. A small amount of garden soil can help to give the right micro-organisms. A layer of nettles or comfrey also helps to add nitrogen to the mix.

Using your compost When the compost is ready, it will be dark brown, light and should smell like good soil. In spring, feed your plants by putting the compost around them as they begin to grow. In autumn, put compost around your plants as a soil conditioner for the winter.

A Visual Dictionary of Brooms and Brushes

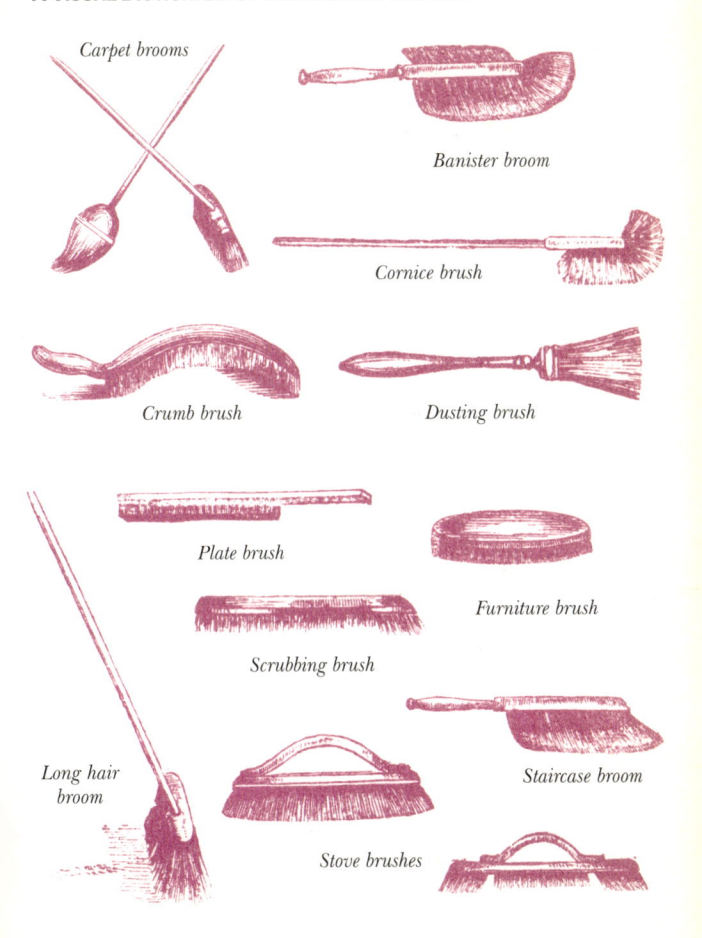

Carpet brooms

Banister broom

Cornice brush

Crumb brush

Dusting brush

Plate brush

Furniture brush

Scrubbing brush

Long hair broom

Staircase broom

Stove brushes

A COMPENDIUM OF HOUSEHOLD HINTS

DELICATE FABRICS AND THEIR CARE

Fabric	Use/Appearance	Care
Broderie anglaise	Cotton fabric with a lacy pattern of small holes	Unless it is very delicate, wash with other cotton garments
Cheesecloth	Lightweight, loosely woven cotton used for shirts, etc	Wash as for non-colourfast cotton; dry carefully so garments keep their shape
Chenille	Soft silk or synthetic with a raised pile; used for curtains, tablecloths and, usually mixed with other fabrics, for clothing	Wash carefully as colours may run; chenille wears out quickly, so handwash or dry clean it
Chiffon	A soft, sheer fabric made from silk or synthetics	For silk or viscose chiffon, dry clean; iron while damp, to keep garment in shape
Crêpe de chine	Thin material with a wrinkly texture and a slight shine, made from silk or viscose	Dry clean or wash in warm water, according to care instructions; iron on the wrong side while damp
Lawn	Very fine, soft cotton	Wash gently and iron on the wrong side
Muslin	Originally used to strain cheese, this loosely woven, thin fabric is now used as a fashion fabric	Wash carefully to retain the garment's shape
Piqué	Cotton or synthetic fabric with a raised design	Iron on the reverse side of the fabric with a thick cloth to stop the pile pattern from flattening out
Voile	A sheer, floating fabric made from cotton, silk or synthetic fibres	Treat according to care instructions; do not wring; iron gently while damp

COFFEE SHOP LINGO

Name of drink	*Meaning*
Amaretto	Espresso with almond syrup
Americano	Espresso diluted with hot water
Americano Misto	Americano with milk
Brève	Espresso with skimmed milk
Café au Lait	French for coffee with boiled milk
Café con Leche	Spanish for espresso with steamed milk
Cappuccino	Espresso with foamed milk
Con Panna	Espresso with whipped cream
Corretto	Espresso with liqueur added
Crème	Espresso with thick cream
Decaf	Decaffeinated coffee, usually latte
Double or Doppio	Double espresso
Espresso	Small shot of very strong black coffee
Frappuccino	Iced cappuccino
Freddo	Iced or chilled espresso
Granita	Espresso with frozen milk
Harmless	Another name for Decaf
Latte	Espresso with steamed and foamed milk
Lungo	Another name for an Americano
Machiato	Espresso with a dash of milk
Medici	Double espresso with chocolate syrup, orange peel and whipped cream
Mocha	Latte with chocolate and whipped cream
Mochaccino	Cappuccino with chocolate
No Fun	Decaf latte, or decaf, non-fat latte
On a Leash	To take away
Shot in the Dark	Regular coffee with a shot of espresso
Skinny	Non-fat or skimmed milk latte
Skinny Harmless	Decaf, non-fat latte
Speed Ball	Another name for Shot in the Dark
Why Bother	Another name for Skinny Harmless

A COMPENDIUM OF HOUSEHOLD HINTS

CAR GAMES FOR KIDS

Thinking up boredom-busting games for restless kids on a long car journey can be a problem. Here are a few games to pass the time:

Arp arp language The players must say their names using 'arp arp' language by putting the syllable arp before each vowel in their name. For example, Jan Brown will be Jarpan Brarpown. John Smith will be Jarpohn Smarpith. Once everyone gets the hang of it, you can conduct arp-arp conversations – e.g. 'Harpellarpo! Harpow arpare yarpou?' or 'Farpine, tharpank yarpou.'

Car scores Each player chooses a car colour. (For older children, different makes of car may be more interesting.) Every time the car colour or make is spotted, the player gets a point. The winner is the player with the highest score.

Cartoon characters Choose a favourite cartoon TV programme and test everyone's knowledge of the characters. This game can range from easy questions for small children (e.g. 'What is the name of the yellow Tellytubby?' or 'What is the name of Homer's son?') to harder ones, such as 'What is the name of the Simpsons' dog?' When a player gets the right answer, it is their turn to think of a character.

Pub cricket The players must look out for pub signs. When someone sees a pub sign, he or she must count the number of legs in the picture. Some will show several legs (e.g. The Coach and Horses), while others will have only two (e.g. The Green Man). Keep scoring until someone spots a pub with no legs (e.g. The Four Barrels). That person is then out and the next player has their turn. The player with the highest number of legs is the winner.

Twenty questions One person thinks of an object, animal or famous person. The others must guess what or who it is by asking questions. You can only answer 'yes' or 'no' to the questions. The player who guesses the answer within 20 questions, then thinks of a subject.

Nuts!

"God gives the nuts but we must crack them ourselves."
(German saying)

This expression means that you must work to get the good things in life, just as you must work to get at the meat of the nut. Ponder this saying as you crack your way through the traditional Christmas bowl of almonds, brazil nuts, hazelnuts and walnuts!

To Hang a Picture

Choose the spot Hanging pictures high will make a room look taller and narrower; hanging them low makes the ceiling seem lower and the room wider.

To hang pictures from a picture hook Make a cross with masking tape at the spot where you want to put your picture hook so that you'll hit the right spot – without making cracks in the plaster when you hammer in the nails.

The right hook Light pictures need small hooks. Large pictures need two hooks. Heavy pictures and mirrors must be mounted securely using heavy gauge screws with rawl plugs. If using two hooks or screws make sure they are horizontally level – a spirit level is the best tool for this.

Straight lines Winding masking tape around the centre of the picture wire will help you to hang the picture straight.

To hang pictures from a picture rail Use new, good quality picture wire for good looks and security.

Raising or lowering a picture Don't move the hook; instead try altering the length of the picture wire until you get it right. If you do need to put in a new nail, don't hammer it in too near your old hole or the plaster may crumble.

Owner and Puppy Training

Puppies are so cute and playful that it is easy to overindulge them. But for the sake of future peace and harmony in your household, it is worth establishing some good habits for you and your puppy from day one. Work on the theory that the puppy sees itself as a member of your family and needs to be constantly reminded of its lowly position in the pack.

- Always walk through doors first before allowing your puppy to walk through. This will show that you are the leader of the pack.
- Give your puppy its own bed and rug. Don't let it climb on the furniture or sleep on your bed as this will make it feel superior.
- Eat something yourself, such as a biscuit, in front of your puppy before feeding it, to signal your higher ranking in the pack. Never feed your puppy at the table; it only encourages it to beg for food.
- If your puppy barks at you for attention, don't respond immediately. Wait before feeding or playing with it or taking it out for a walk.
- When your puppy jumps up to greet people, encourage them to ignore it. Alternatively, tell them to say 'down', and pat the puppy while keeping the palm of your hand flat on its back or head to indicate that it must not jump up.
- A young puppy often bites and nips when playing. Say 'Ouch' in a loud voice and discontinue the game if it keeps biting.
- Train your puppy to come back to you on a word of command or a whistle. Keep small food treats in your pocket to give as a reward and praise it with lots of pats and cuddles when it obeys you.
- Take your puppy to a dog obedience class. Not only will it learn to sit, wait, stay and walk to heel on command, but just as importantly it will socialise with other dogs. Most vets will have information on where to find a class in your area.

DRESSMAKING TERMS

Aglet	The metal tag on the end of a lace
Crimp	Gather or crease in a regular pattern
Eyelet	A small hole edged with metal or buttonhole stitch, for threading a lace through
Facing	A section of fabric sewn inside the edge of a garment: e.g. an armhole, to form a neat lining
Fancy work	Needlework with embroidery stitches used to decorate a garment
French chalk	Chalk for marking a pattern cut onto fabric
Goose	a heavy iron with a sharp nose, used by tailors to press garments
Gore, gusset	A wedge-shaped piece inserted into a garment such as a skirt or pair of trousers, to enlarge it
Placket	A slit down the side of a skirt or pair of trousers, closed by a zip or other kind of fastening
Rever	A lapel, showing the lining or inside of the garment
Tack	To hold together lightly with a large stitch before sewing properly
Tuck	A pleat held in place by stitching
Vent	A small opening at the bottom of a garment, usually at the bottom of the back
Waxed cotton	Thread rubbed with wax to keep it from knotting
Yoke	The upper section of a garment, either the front from neck to chest or the back from neck to shoulder blades

SHOWER FRESH

To get spots and mildew out of plastic shower curtains, put them in the washing machine with *140g (5oz) of detergent* and *250ml (8fl oz) of distilled malt vinegar*. Add one or two old towels to the wash. Put the washing machine on a medium cycle and when it is done, hang the shower curtain back on the shower rail to dry.

A COMPENDIUM OF HOUSEHOLD HINTS

FAVOURITE SCREEN CLEANERS

Star	Film	Date	Chore
Julie Andrews	*Mary Poppins*	1964	Tidying nursery
Annette Bening	*American Beauty*	1999	Vacuuming
Joan Blondell	*Dames*	1934	Ironing
Bette Davis	*The Star*	1952	Cleaning kitchen
Jane Fonda	*The Morning After*	1986	Post-murder cleaning
Judy Garland	*Till the Clouds Roll By*	1946	Washing dishes
Diane Keaton	*Baby Boom*	1987	Making baby food
Jack Lemmon	*The Odd Couple*	1968	Compulsive tidying
Jennifer Lopez	*Maid in Manhattan*	2002	Cleaning hotel rooms
Kathleen Turner	*Serial Mom*	1994	Constant cleaning
Dick van Dyke	*Mary Poppins*	1964	Cleaning chimneys

GRASPING THE NETTLE

Tender-handed stroke a nettle,
And it stings you for your pains;
Grasp it like a man of mettle,
And it soft as silk remains.

Aaron Hill (1685–1750)
English poet and dramatist

THE FIRST TEA-TIME

The fine 'old' custom of afternoon tea is, in fact, not that ancient at all. It is credited to the Duchess of Bedford (1788–1861), who began to invite friends over in the late afternoon for a light meal at 5pm. At the time, people ate only twice a day and would often face an uncomfortable 'grumbling' stomach in between meals.

WEATHER LORE
It is still believed by many that if hedgerow plants produce a profusion of berries, it will be a hard winter:

> *The thorns and briars, vermillion-hue,*
> *Now full of hips and haws are seen;*
> *If village prophecies be true,*
> *They prove that winter will be keen.*
>
> Autumn: John Clare (1793–1864)

HOLY TIPPLES
For centuries, monks have brewed strong alcoholic liqueurs. They are now sold around the world. Benedictine and Chartreuse are the most popular. Chartreuse has many varieties and was once called 'the elixir of life'.

Liqueur	*Monastic order*
Aiguebelle	Cistercian
Benedictine	Benedictine
Carmeline	Cistercian
Chartreuse	Carthusian
Frangelico	Fra Angelico, early monk
La Senancole	Cistercian
Trappastine	Cistercian

A FENG SHUI TIP FOR TROPICAL FISH OWNERS
Be careful where you place a fish tank. If you place it correctly – facing where you work or near the front door – you will have good fortune, but the wrong position – behind your back where you work or by the back door – will bring you money troubles.

TO REMOVE BIRO MARKS FROM CLOTHES
Pen marks on clothing can sometimes be removed by putting a few drops of alcohol-based perfume into the fabric – but first test on a hidden part of the fabric to check that the perfume doesn't stain it.

Tropical Fish for Beginners

Danios *e.g. Blue, Giant, Pearl, Zebra*
Danios are good for beginners as they are some of the easiest fish to breed in an aquarium.

Goldfish *e.g. Bubble Eyes, Orandas, Ranchus*
Goldfish are good starter fish. They come in many colours, with a variety of tail, body and head shapes, and telescoped eyes.

Guppies *e.g. Kwartler, Miller, Paluna, Roebuck, Ted Dix*
Guppies are an excellent fish to buy for children, or for people just starting to keep tropical fish in an aquarium.

Scavengers *e.g. Algae Eater, Clown Loach, Kuhil Loach, Placostemous, Rainbow Shark, Redtail Shark, Spotted Corydoras, Striped Corydoras*
Scavengers and catfish are useful because they eat up left-over food and decaying plants, helping to keep the water clean.

Tetras *Black, Bleeding Heart, Bloodfin, Cardinal, Congo, Emperor, Glowlight, Green, Head-Taillight, Lemon, Neon, Serpae*
Tetras are easy to keep, but are more difficult to breed than most other tropical fish. They are happier when living in schools of about six fish or more.

Honey Bees

When choosing honey, it might be worth following the bees' lead.

The pedigree of honey
Does not concern the bee;
A clover, any time, to him
Is aristocracy.

Emily Dickinson (1830–86)

CONVERT YOUR WEIGHT TO AND FROM KILOGRAMS

Kilograms	Stones/Pounds	Pounds
48	7st 8lb	106
50	7st 12lb	110
52	8st 3lb	115
54	8st 7lb	119
56	8st 11lb	123
58	9st 2lb	128
60	9st 6lb	132
62	9st 11lb	137
64	10st 1lb	141
66	10st 6lb	146
68	10st 10lb	150
70	11st 0lb	154
72	11st 5lb	159
74	11st 9lb	163
76	12st 0lb	168
78	12st 4lb	172
80	12st 8lb	176
82	12st 13lb	181
84	13st 3lb	185
86	13st 8lb	190
88	13st 12lb	194
90	14st 2lb	198
92	14st 7lb	203
94	14st 11lb	207
96	15st 0lb	212

KEEP IT FIZZY

To keep the fizz in an opened bottle of champagne, put a teaspoon into the neck of the bottle. Take it out to pour the champagne, then replace it until the bottle is empty. The metal reacts with gases to keep bubbles in the liquid.

A COMPENDIUM OF HOUSEHOLD HINTS

DRESSING FOR DINNER

For a formal dinner party, dress should be severe rather than fluffy. Fuss and frills are out of place at dinner parties.

STRAWBERRY BANANA SMOOTHIE

You will need a good blender to make any kind of smoothie.

To whiz up this one for two people, slice *6 strawberries* and *1 banana* and drop them into the blender with *250ml (8fl oz) of natural yogurt*, *250ml (8fl oz) of orange juice* and a *handful of ice cubes*. Blitz the ingredients until mixture has a smooth, thick consistency. Pour into cold glasses and serve at once for a nourishing breakfast or refreshing snack at any time of the day.

☆ Using frozen strawberries instead of ice will produce a thicker smoothie. In fact, it is a good idea to keep a small supply of frozen fruit in the freezer for making smoothies whenever you want them.

☆ Making a smoothie is a good way to use up bananas that have become too ripe for eating – they mash down well and make the tastiest smoothies.

COUNTING MAGPIES

The omens depend on the number of magpies
you see together at one time:

One for sorrow,
Two for mirth;
Three a wedding,
Four a birth;
Five for silver,
Six for gold,
Seven for a secret, not to be told;
Eight for Heaven,
Nine for Hell,
And Ten for the devil's ain sel'.

Smoothing out the Creases
- Iron bed linen and clothes while they are still slightly damp from the clothes line or tumble dryer. This makes it easier to get the creases out.
- If necessary, dampen an item with water from a spray gun or from the spray button on your iron. The old-fashioned method of dipping your hand in a bowl of water and flicking it over the garment before ironing also works.
- Damp cotton and linen should be ironed right side up, as these fabrics crease easily.
- Iron glazed cotton on the right side to add sheen.
- After ironing, air the laundry on a clothes horse or in the airing cupboard until completely dry before putting it away.

Being the Perfect Host
- Your aim should be to create a warm, comfortable and relaxed setting in which your guests feel welcome and can enjoy their meal in pleasant company, accompanied by some stimulating conversation.
- Try to give the impression that you have taken some trouble and care with the meal, but don't make your guests feel uncomfortable with arrangements that are too fussy and formal.
- Plan ahead and try to think of everything that your guests will need for the meal in advance, so that you can relax and enjoy the occasion, too, rather than having to rush around all the time.

What's Inside a Housemaid's Box?
The housemaid carried a wooden box filled with all the tools she would need to clean the fireplaces: black-lead brushes, leathers, emery paper, cloth and black lead. Her first chore at the start of every day would be to clean all the fireplaces in the house and to light fires in the rooms that would be used during the day.

A COMPENDIUM OF HOUSEHOLD HINTS

TABLE LAYING
When you are setting a table for a formal meal:

❖ Lay felt or a thick cloth underneath a tablecloth to stop it slipping and to protect the table.

❖ Place a large heat-proof mat under the tablecloth.

❖ Either fold the napkins, or roll them up and put them in rings. Then place the napkins to the left of each place setting on a small sideplate, which will later be used for bread or rolls.

MAKING MORE ELBOW ROOM
If your table is rather small for the number of people you want to seat around it, serve some dishes, such as carved meat, vegetables or desserts from a sideboard or another smaller table.

FLOWERS ON THE DINING TABLE
A vase of fresh flowers, or other table decoration, always looks nice in the centre of the table. However, make sure your arrangement is not too tall, otherwise guests will have to peer round it or it may be knocked over when people are passing food.

ARRANGING THE CUTLERY
When laying each place setting, place the cutlery in order of use:

❖ Put a soup spoon on the outside to the right, as it will be used first.

❖ Then put a fish knife and fork, followed by a meat knife and fork and, lastly, a cheese knife.

❖ A dessert knife or spoon and fork can be placed at the top of the plate or can be laid immediately to the left and right of the plate, in sequence with the rest of the cutlery.

TWO OR MORE GLASSES

❖ Follow the rule that the glass to be used first should be nearest the hand. You may want to set one glass for the white wine to be served with the starter, one for red wine to accompany the main course and a glass for water poured from a jug or decorative bottle on the table.

❖ To avoid cluttering the table, leave smaller glasses for dessert wine and after-dinner port, brandy or liqueurs on the side and only put them on the table with dessert or coffee.

Port *Champagne* *Claret*

SERVING ACCOMPANIMENTS

❖ Put butter on a dish with a small silver butter knife. A tiny sprig of parsley on top of the butter looks nice.

❖ Put a cold sauce or dressing in a dish or jug and stand it on a small plate or saucer with a spoon beside it.

❖ Hand round gravy in a gravy boat when you serve the meat, to ensure it will be hot.

❖ Make sure salt, pepper and mustard are available to your guests. If the table is large, use a couple of sets, one at each end.

❖ If you are serving cream with the dessert, put it in a small jug or bowl on a saucer. Don't forget to provide a spoon, especially if the cream is thick.

❖ Arrange coffee cups, spoons, coffee pot, cream, milk and sugar on a tray, so that you can serve coffee quickly at the end of the meal.

Liqueur *Tumbler* *Sherry*

A COMPENDIUM OF HOUSEHOLD HINTS

BOILING POINT
At high altitudes, water and other liquids boil at a lower temperature than at sea level. A liquid's boiling point depends on the atmospheric pressure pushing down on its surface. Since there is less atmospheric pressure at higher altitudes, the boiling point will be lower on top of Ben Nevis than in the Norfolk Broads. So at high altitudes food needs to be kept over heat longer in order to cook. At 2,125m (7,000ft), for example, dried beans will take twice as long to cook as at sea level. Here are the boiling temperatures for various altitudes.

Altitude	*Centigrade*	*Farenheit*
Sea level	100°	212°
610m (2,000ft)	98°	208°
1,525m (5,000ft)	95°	203°
2,285m (7,500ft)	92°	198°
3,050m (10,000ft)	90°	195°
4,570m (15,000ft)	85°	185°

FREEZER STAR SYMBOLS
Frozen foods are marked with star symbols which indicate how long they will keep in an ordinary home freezer.

* One week
** Up to one month.
*** Up to three months.

WHAT A SCORCHER!
❖ Soak fabric overnight in cold water to remove recent scorch marks.
❖ White fabrics that have been scorched can sometimes be bleached back to their original colour.

FRESH AS A LEMON
Put fresh lemons in a jar or bowl of cold water. Lemons stored in this way will keep fresh for up to a month if you change the water often.

HOW MANY SPOONFULS MAKE AN OUNCE?

Use a British standard tablespoon instead of scales to measure out 1oz (25gm). These ingredients, measured in level tablespoons, weigh about 1oz.

Number of spoonfuls	Ingredient
3	Breadcrumbs (dry)
6	Breadcrumbs (fresh)
5	Cheese (grated)
4	Cocoa powder
5	Coconut (desiccated)
2	Currants, raisins and sultanas
4	Nuts (ground)
4	Porridge oats
2	Rice
1	Salt
3	Semolina, flour, custard powder and cornflour
3	Sugar, demerara and icing sugar (sifted)
2	Sugar, granulated and caster
1	Syrup, honey, treacle and jam

CARE OF LINEN FABRICS

Linen is a hardwearing fabric woven from a natural fibre – flax. It is used for making curtains, upholstery and clothing.
- It may shrink if washed at high temperatures.
- It creases badly unless mixed with synthetic fibres.
- To remove creases, press with a hot iron while still damp.

TO CLEAN ARTIFICIAL FLOWERS

Put fabric flowers in a plastic bag with *30ml (2tbsp) of salt*. Shake the bag and the salt will clean off the dust. Alternatively, using a hair dryer on a cool setting removes dust from fabric flowers and also from dried flower arrangements. To avoid spraying dust on to the wall behind the flowers; first move the vase into a different place.

A COMPENDIUM OF HOUSEHOLD HINTS

HOW TO PLAY BEANS ARE HOT
One player is chosen to be sent out of the room by flipping a coin. A person or article is hidden in the room. The kept out of the room is called in with the chant: 'Hot beans and melted butter, please my lady/master, come to supper'. The player moves about the room; when he or she is close to the hidden article, the other players yell 'hot beans'. When he or she moves away from it, they call out, 'cold beans', until the person or article is found.

STALE BISCUITS AND CEREAL
You can perk up unappetising soggy biscuits or stale cereal by laying them on a baking sheet and putting them in a hot oven for a few minutes. This method also works if you heat them in the microwave for half a minute.

VANILLA VACUUMING
Soak a cotton puff in vanilla extract, then drop it into your vacuum cleaner bag – the vanilla scent will be blown out of the vacuum cleaner's exhaust, perfuming your home.

MANGO SMOOTHIE
This delicious smoothie is based on the Indian *mango lassi*, a cool, refreshing drink for hot weather or to serve with spicy curries.

For two people, peel and slice *1 ripe mango* and tip it into the blender with *250ml (8fl oz) of natural yogurt, 250ml (8fl oz) of water, 2.5ml (½tsp) of cinnamon* and *a pinch of cardamom*. Zap everything together until it is as smooth as you want and runny enough to drink through a large straw. Serve with a garnish of fresh mango slices and a sprig of mint.

☆ To thicken, add a scoop of ice cream or a handful of ice cubes.

☆ To thin it down, add more water or some milk. Only pour in a little at a time or your smoothie may become too runny.

CLOTHES CLEANING KIT

Detergents
Biological and heavy-duty liquid detergents.

Glycerine
Available from the chemist. Softens waxy, dried-in and sticky stains. Use diluted 1 part to 2 parts water. Apply to garment and leave for 1 hour before washing as normal.

Hydrogen peroxide
Ask your chemist for the type that is 20 per cent by volume. Mix 1 part to 6 parts water and soak for 30 minutes until the stain has cleared.

Lighter fluid
Apply neat with cotton wool to remove chewing gum or glue from synthetic fabrics.

Methylated spirits
Try to purchase the colourless type from the chemist. Apply with cotton wool buds to remove biro marks, chewing gum or glue.

Pre-wash stain remover
Sold as solid bars, liquid or sprays.

White spirit
Use neat, dabbed on to grease stains. First test for colour fastness in an inconspicuous spot.

There are no hard and fast rules for stain removal:
- ◆ Always test the fabric first in an inconspicuous area.
- ◆ Chemical treatments can further damage a fabric weakened by age.

A COMPENDIUM OF HOUSEHOLD HINTS

How to Store a Wedding Gown

- Have someone take your wedding gown to the cleaners as soon as possible after the event. Don't wait until you come back from your honeymoon when the stains will have had time to set.
- Look over the dress to identify any stains and bring them to the attention of your dry cleaner. Give your dry cleaner any instructions for cleaning the dress that came with it.
- After cleaning, pack the gown in a large storage box with non-acid tissue paper. Stuff the bodice and sleeves with tissue paper. A dry cleaner who specialises in wedding dresses can pack it for you.
- Store shoes, veil and accessories in separate boxes or bags.
- Do not store anything in plastic, because it causes yellowing.
- Store in a cool, dry place. Most lofts are too hot, while most cellars are too damp.

Eating Fruit

Different rules apply when you are eating fruit as a dessert at the dining table than when you are having a quick fruity snack.

- ✔ Eat grapes with your fingers. Snip or break a small cluster of grapes from the larger bunch and place it on your plate. Do not pull individual grapes from the big bunch.
- ✔ Peel a banana and cut it into slices or break it into small pieces that you can eat with your fingers.
- ✔ To eat an apple, peel it with a sharp knife or not as you prefer. Then cut it into slices and eat these with your fingers.
- ✔ Completely remove the skin from an orange and divide it into segments. Do not cut the orange into quarters and suck on each section like a sports person during the halftime break.
- ✔ Eat juicy fruits such as pears, peaches and pineapple with a fruit knife and fork.
- ✔ Take fruit stones and pips out of your mouth with a spoon, a fork or your fingers and place them discreetly on the side of your plate. Refrain from spitting them straight out on to the plate.

EATING DIFFICULT FOODS

✔ Eat your soup off the side of the spoon, with the soup bowl tilted away from you.

✘ Don't suck and slurp noisily from the spoon.

✔ Eat corn on the cob by inserting the two little forks, if provided, at each end of the cob. Then rotate the cob and nibble the corn from it as elegantly as you can.

✘ Don't pick up the cob with your fingers, unless eating outdoors at a picnic.

✔ Eat barbecued meat with your fingers outdoors.

✘ Don't eat barbecued meat with your fingers indoors. Use a knife and fork.

✔ Ask how to eat something if you are unsure. There is nothing wrong with not knowing how to tackle a globe artichoke or a lobster, for example. Many of the rules vary from country to country anyway.

✘ Don't order food in a restaurant that is difficult to eat or with you which are totally unfamiliar, if you think it will make you nervous.

✔ Eat spaghetti by twisting the strands around your fork. Some people find it easier to balance the fork on a spoon while doing this to help guide the spaghetti.

✘ Don't stuff long strands of spaghetti into your mouth and slurp them up noisily.

✔ Remove bones from chicken and fish from your mouth with a fork.

✘ Don't pick up chicken or fish bones with your hands.

SILK FABRICS AND THEIR CARE

Silk is a delicate natural fibre of varying weight and quality.

- It is normally handwashed, but dry clean particularly fine or decorated silks.
- Do not wring. Lay the item between two towels to absorb the water.
- Perspiration stains are difficult to remove, but sometimes disappear after dry cleaning.
- Do not spray with water while ironing, otherwise water marks can appear. Re-dampen the whole garment.

Fabric	Use/Appearance	Care
Satin	A shiny, smooth fabric traditionally made from silk, but now more often from synthetic fibres	Wash according to fibre, but dry clean heavy satin; iron on the wrong side while damp, to maintain the shiny finish
Shantung	Originally raw silk with uneven, bobbly threads, now often made with synthetic fibres	Wash as for silk or synthetics and iron on wrong side when garment is completely dry
Taffeta	A stiff, rustling fabric often used for skirts and dresses; originally made from silk, but now often mixed with synthetics	Wash according to the fabric type, or dry clean; hang the garment up to drip dry and iron on the wrong side while damp

SNIFTER OF BRANDY

A snifter is a pear-shaped glass with a short stem used for serving brandy and cognacs. The bowl should be held in the palm of the hand, to warm up the drink. This will slightly release the delicious aroma that is trapped by the narrow neck, thereby enhancing the enjoyment of the imbiber.

CHOOSING FRESH FISH

To make sure the fish you buy is fresh, buy it from a busy fishmonger. The shop should not smell fishy! Buy the fish on the day you plan to cook it – domestic fridges aren't cold enough to store fish. Use all your senses when shopping. Look for:

- Fish that smells sweet and fresh, like the sea.
- Clear, bright eyes, rather than red and sunken.
- Flesh that is firm to the touch, not flabby.
- Clean and shiny, not dull and slimy, skin.
- Pink gills – they should not be brown or red.
- No red or brown areas, or pink spots on the body: these are bruises.

CHAMPAGNE GLASSES

Champagne is served in many different kinds of glass.

Coup: a saucer-shaped glass, with a shallow bowl on a long stem.
Flute: tall and narrow all the way up, helping to trap bubbles and keep in 'fizz'.
Goblet: a small version of the water goblet.
Hollow: has a hollow stem, which creates a fountain of bubbles from the middle of the glass.
Trumpet: a tall, slender glass that is narrow at the base.

POST 'ACCIDENT' CARPET CARE

If your pet has an 'accident' on a carpet, mop or clean it up, then wash the area with a carpet cleaner to remove the stain. Finally, to get rid of the lingering odour, sprinkle with bicarbonate of soda, leave for an hour, then vacuum. If that doesn't work, *mix 250ml (8fl oz) of distilled malt vinegar and 250ml (8fl oz) of water* in a spray bottle and spray the area until it is really wet. After three days, both the smell of vinegar and of urine will be gone.

LIQUID MEASURES

1 teaspoon (5ml)	=	1 teaspoon
1 tablespoon (15ml)	=	1 tablespoon
120ml	=	4fl oz
150ml	=	¼pt = 5fl oz
175ml	=	6fl oz
200ml	=	⅓pt = 7fl oz
250ml	=	8fl oz
300ml	=	½pt = 10fl oz
350ml	=	12fl oz
400ml	=	14fl oz
450ml	=	¾pt = 15fl oz
500ml	=	18fl oz
600ml	=	1pt = 20fl oz
750ml	=	1¼pt
900ml	=	1½pt
1 litre	=	1¾pt
1.2 litres	=	2pt
1.25 litres	=	2¼pt
1.5 litres	=	2½pt
1.6 litres	=	2¾pt
1.75 litres	=	3pt
2 litres	=	3½pt
2.25 litres	=	4pt
2.5 litres	=	4½pt
2.75 litres	=	5pt

USING AMERICAN MEASURES

In American cookery, some measures that cooks use are different from those used in Britain (e.g. where a pint is equal to 20fl oz):

1 pint	=	16fl oz
1 cup	=	8fl oz

MILES PER GALLON – MILES PER LITRE

50 miles to 1 gallon	=	11.0 miles to 1 litre
40 miles to 1 gallon	=	8.8 miles to 1 litre
30 miles to 1 gallon	=	6.6 miles to 1 litre
20 miles to 1 gallon	=	4.4 miles to 1 litre

SMELL BUSTERS

- To cover the smell of burnt food in the house, boil a few slices of lemon in a saucepan of water.
- When frying food, a saucer of distilled malt vinegar placed by the cooker will help clear the air.
- A mixture of brown sugar and cinnamon baked in the oven on a very low heat for a minimum of half an hour will help to make your house smell warm and inviting.
- One or two cloves simmered in a saucepan of water helps to keep air humid in the house and adds a pleasant smell.
- For unpleasant smells in the bathroom, light a match or two. The flame literally burns away the gases.

SOAK AWAY STAINS

Use denture-cleaning tablets to take out stains from white linen and cotton. Dissolve a tablet in *140ml (4fl oz) of water* and pour it over the stain. Then wash the item in hot water.

KEEP HOUSEPLANTS KITTY FREE

Sprinkle a spoonful of ground coffee on to the soil on top of each pot plant. Cats hate the smell and will stay away, while plants benefit from the nutrients in the coffee grounds.

DEPARTMENT OF LOST SOCKS

To prevent socks getting separated in the wash, pin pairs together with a safety pin. You can leave the pin in while washing, tumble drying or hanging on a clothesline. Pin the socks at the top so they will dry quickly.

A COMPENDIUM OF HOUSEHOLD HINTS

RAT POISON
A good way of poisoning rats is to cut down some corks into thin pieces and stew them in grease. When the rats eat the corks, they will die of indigestion.

WASHING WHITES AND COLOUREDS TOGETHER
When washing coloured clothes, put an old white handkerchief or rag in with the wash to see if it picks up any colour from the other clothes. If it stays white, your coloured items have stopped losing dye and you can wash them with white clothes. However, make sure you wash them at the same temperature – the colour may still run if they are washed at a higher temperature.

BIRTH DAYS
- Monday's child is fair of face
- Tuesday's child is full of grace
- Wednesday's child is full of woe
- Thursday's child has far to go
- Friday's child is loving and giving
- Saturday's child works hard for a living
- But the child that is born on the Sabbath day
  Is bonny and blithe, and good and gay.

FREE-FLOWING DRAINS
To keep drains clear, pour *310g (11oz) of bicarbonate of soda* and *310g (11oz) of salt* down it, followed by *a kettleful of hot water*. Don't use the drain for several hours. This will dissolve any grease in the drain.

SMELLY TRAINERS
To freshen up smelly trainers, fill them with clean cat litter and leave overnight. In the morning, shake out the cat litter from the insides of the trainers into a plastic bag and throw the bag away. Your shoes will smell nice and fresh again.

PECTIN AND ACID CHART FOR MAKING JAM

Some fruits are naturally high in pectin (see below) and when boiled with sugar, form a gel which makes the jam set. If the fruit you are making your jam with is low in pectin, either add pectin or use sugar with added pectin which is sold in most supermarkets. If the fruit is low in acid, you will need to add lemon juice. Your jam recipe will give the exact amounts.

Fruit	Pectin	Acidity
Apples	* * *	* *
Apricots	* *	* *
Blackberries	* *	* *
Blackcurrants	* * *	* * *
Blueberries	* *	* *
Cherries	*	* *
Cranberries	* * *	* *
Damsons	* * *	* * *
Elderberries	*	*
Figs	*	*
Gooseberries	* * *	* * *
Grapefruit	* * *	* * *
Grapes	* *	* *
Greengages	* *	* * *
Lemons and limes	* * *	* * *
Mangoes	*	*
Passion fruit	*	* *
Peaches	*	*
Pears	*	*
Pineapples	*	* *
Plums	* * *	* * *
Quinces	* * *	*
Raspberries	* *	* *
Redcurrants	* * *	* * *
Rhubarb	*	* * *
Seville oranges	* * *	* * *
Strawberries	*	*
Sweet oranges	* * *	* *
Tangerines	* *	* *

Key: * * * *high* * * *moderate* * *low*

SUGAR BOILING

The texture of a sugar syrup once it has cooled depends on the temperature to which it was first boiled. The higher the temperature, the more moisture is driven off and the harder it will set. The temperature bands, their names and how to test them are as follows:

SOFT BALL
Fondant
Fudge

112–116°C (234–240°F)
A small spoonful of syrup dropped into ice water forms a soft, sticky ball when you roll it in your fingers.

FIRM BALL
Soft caramels

118–121°C (244–250°F)
A small spoonful of syrup dropped into ice water will form a firm but still rather sticky ball, which loses its shape quite quickly when out of the water.

HARD BALL
Marshmallow
Nougat

121–130°C (250–266°F)
A small spoonful of syrup dropped into ice water will quickly form a ball which, although sticky and pliable, does hold its shape out of water.

SOFT CRACK
Butterscotch
Toffee

132–143°C (270–290°F)
A small spoonful of syrup dropped into ice water is firm to the touch when you take it out and can be stretched and bent into pliable strands.

HARD CRACK
Barley sugar
Fruit drops
Hard toffee

149–154°C (300–310°F)
A small spoonful of syrup dropped into ice water forms stiff threads when removed. It snaps easily and will not be sticky.

CARAMEL
Brittle
Praline

160–177°C (320–350°F)
Smells deliciously of caramel. Colour is the other distinguishing factor. It can range from pale gold to rich chestnut, but should not be darker or the caramel will be more bitter than sweet.

U AND NON-U

A person's social class is often evident simply by the words he or she uses. For example, those who watch television in the sitting room are upper class (U), while those who do their viewing in the lounge are of a lower social class (non-U).

The terms 'U' and 'non-U' were jokingly coined to describe the language use of the upper and lower classes of British society in *Noblesse Oblige*, a book of essays edited by British aristocrat Nancy Mitford and published in 1956.

U	*Non-U*
chimney piece	mantelpiece
die	pass away
Esq.	Mr (when addressing a letter)
grandmother	nanny, nan
'How do you do?'	'Pleased to meet you'
knife and fork	cutlery
lavatory	toilet
looking glass	mirror
lunch, luncheon	dinner
motor car	car
napkin	serviette
omnibus	bus
pudding	dessert, sweet, afters
salt and pepper	cruet
scent	perfume
sitting room	lounge
sofa	settee
supper or dinner	tea
telephone	phone
What? / I beg your pardon?	pardon
writing paper	notepaper

DEEP-FRYING TIMES AND TEMPERATURES

All kinds of food can be battered or breaded and then deep fried – from savoury items such as chicken, veal and fish to snacks such as doughnuts, potato crisps and onion rings. Fry food in batches and make sure the pieces are the same size.

Food	Time	Temperature
Cheese beignets	6–8 min	190°C (375°F)
Chicken drumsticks	15–20 min	180°C (350°F)
Chicken Kiev	10–15 min	180°C (350°F)
Chips		
1cm (½in) thick	10 min	190°C (375°F)
Croquettes	1–2 min	190°C (375°F)
Doughnuts		
(ring)	2–3 min	190°C (375°F)
(ball)	2–3 min	190°C (375°F)
Fish fillets	7–12 min	180°C (350°F)
Fritters	1–2 min	190°C (375°F)
Matchstick potatoes	1–2 min	190°C (375°F)
Onion rings	2–3 min	190°C (375°F)
Potato crisps	1–2 min	190°C (375°F)
Samosas	8–12 min	180°C (350°F)
Veal escalopes	3–5 min	200°C (400°F)
Whitebait	1–2 min	190°C (375°F)

FIXING A STICKY ZIP

A zip that is stuck can sometimes be loosened by applying a little soap on to the teeth, on both the back and the front sides of the zip. This will help to lubricate it so that it starts to work again. If any of the fabric has got caught up in the teeth of the zip, pull it gently out of the teeth without tearing it.

Addressing Servants
The way servants were addressed reflected their status in the household:
- *Butlers* were called by their surnames by the masters and mistresses of the house, but were called 'Mr' by the other servants. Thus Bertie Wooster called his butler 'Jeeves', but the other servants would have called him 'Mr Jeeves'.
- *Cooks* had the reputation of being temperamental, so a good cook was treated with the greatest respect; otherwise she might leave. Cooks were referred to as Miss or Mrs (Surname) or sometimes as 'Cook'.
- *Housemaids* were general maids with specific duties, and they were called by their Christian names.
- *Parlourmaids* presided over meals in households with no butler or footman. They were addressed by their surnames to denote their superior status.
- *Tweenies* were the lowest, least trained servants who went 'between floors' doing fairly unskilled work of all kinds. They were addressed by their Christian names.

Old-fashioned Lemonade
Thinly pare the rind from *two lemons*. Put the rind into a jug with *170g (6oz) of sugar*. Pour over *900ml (1½pt) of boiling water*. Let it cool; then strain the liquid into a large glass jug. Add *300ml (½pt) of sherry* and the *juice of 4 lemons*. Now it's ready to drink. For a non-alcoholic lemonade, substitute water for the sherry. This recipe makes *1.5 litre (2½pt) of lemonade*.

How to Remove Pet Hair from Upholstery
If vacuuming doesn't work, wipe down the furniture while wearing rubber gloves and you'll find the fur will come away on your gloved hands. Pet hair will also come off if you wipe the furniture with a damp sponge or a used sheet of fabric softener.

A–Z OF COMPANION PLANTS

Planting certain flowers, herbs and vegetables together improves soil quality and protects your plants from pests and diseases.

Basil	Plant with tomatoes to repel thrips and flies.
Borage	Plant with tomatoes and strawberries to deter insects and improve soil.
Catnip	Plant with all kinds of flowers and vegetables to deter beetles, aphids, ants and weevils.
Chervil	Plant with radishes and lettuces to improve flavour and keep off aphids.
Chives	Plant among apple trees to prevent scab; improves flavour of carrots and tomatoes.
Chrysanthemum	Kills off all kinds of root-eating pests.
Comfrey	Plant near flowers to attract slugs away from them.
Dahlia	Plant in flowerbeds to kill off pests of all kinds.
Garlic	Plant near roses to keep away aphids; repels beetles, snails, maggots and white flies, as well as fungal diseases.
Larkspur	Plant in flowerbeds; certain beetles eat them and die.
Marigold	Plant in flowerbeds to discourage insects, especially whiteflies – but beware, they attract slugs.
Nasturtium	Plant with vegetables to deter pests and attract aphids, which will eat the nasturtiums, not the vegetables.
Parsley	Plant around the base of roses to increase their fragrance.
Petunia	Plant with tomatoes to repel beetles, aphids and pests.
Rosemary	Plant with vegetables to deter moths, beetles and flies.
Sunflower	Plant near flowers to attract aphids away from them; the aphids will not do the sunflowers much damage.
White geranium	Plant with other flowers to attract certain kinds of beetles, which die after eating the leaves.

ROASTING TIMES AND TEMPERATURES FOR PORK AND LAMB

		Combined High and Low Heat	*Slow-roast*
PORK		Sear at 200°C/400°F/Gas 6 for 10 mins then reduce the heat to 160°C/325°F/Gas 3	
Loin	On the bone	*Medium* 25 min per per 450g (1lb)	
Hand	On the bone	*Medium* 30 min per per 450g (1lb)	
Leg		*Well-done* 35 min per 450g (1lb)	
Shoulder	Off the bone		
Loin	Off the bone		
Leg	Boned and rolled or stuffed	Well-done 35–40 min per 450g (1lb)	
Shoulder			
LAMB		(Sear at 230°C/450°F/Gas 8 for 10 min, then reduce the heat to 180°C/350°F/Gas 4)	(150°C/300°F/Gas 2 for total roasting time)
Best end			
Crown roast		*Rare* 10 min per 450g (1lb)	
Guard of honour	On the bone	*Medium* 12–15 min per 450g (1lb)	
Loin		*Well-done* 20 min per 450g (1lb)	
Saddle			
Shoulder			
Shoulder	Boned and rolled or stuffed		Well-done 35–40 min per 450g (1lb)
Rolled breast			

A COMPENDIUM OF HOUSEHOLD HINTS

WEIGHTS

Here is a handy guide for any cooks who may require a quick conversion table, particularly if using a non-metric cookery book.

15g	=	½oz		400g	=	14oz
20g	=	¾oz		425g	=	15oz
30g	=	1oz		450g	=	1lb
55g	=	2oz		500g	=	1lb 2oz
85g	=	3oz		570g	=	1¼lb
100g	=	3½oz		680g	=	1½lb
110g	=	4oz		900g	=	2lb
140g	=	5oz		1kg	=	2lb 3oz
170g	=	6oz		1.35kg	=	3lb
200g	=	7oz		1.8kg	=	4lb
225g	=	8oz		2.3kg	=	5lb
255g	=	9oz		2.7kg	=	6lb
285g	=	10oz		3.2kg	=	7lb
310g	=	11oz		3.4kg	=	8lb
340g	=	12oz		4kg	=	9lb
370g	=	13oz		4.5kg	=	10lb

GETTING RID OF ANTS THE NATURAL WAY

Ants in the kitchen? Don't want to use pesticides near food? Try this easy three-step plan!

1 Deprive them of food. Do not leave any food or crumbs out on surfaces, particularly in hot weather. Keep food in the fridge or in sealed containers. Don't forget to keep the floor crumb-free and pet dishes clean.

2 Lock them out! Try to find out where they are coming in, and seal all crevices with putty or cement.

3 Fight back. Hang sprigs of penny royal, tansy or rue in kitchen cupboards, sprinkle chilli powder or dried mint across ant trails, or plant a container of mint near the door and under windows.

GUIDE TO GRILLING TIMES FOR FISH

Type of fish	Grilling time
Cod (steak)	5–6 min each side
Dover sole (whole)	4–6 min each side
Dover sole (fillet)	2–3 min each side
Halibut (steak)	5–6 min each side
Herring (whole)	4–5 min each side
Mackerel (whole)	6–7 min each side
Monkfish (steak)	5–6 min each side
Plaice (whole)	4–6 min each side
Plaice (fillet)	2–3 min each side
Salmon (steak)	5–6 min each side
Swordfish (steak)	4–6 min each side
Tuna (steak)	1–2 min each side

Times given for fish weighing approximately 170–225g (6–8oz).

RESHAPING STRETCHED CUFFS

If cuffs on an old jumper have stretched out of shape, wet them with hot water and dry them with a hairdryer on maximum heat setting. This should shrink the wool and the cuffs will go back to their original shape.

SPOON MEASURES

1 tablespoon	=	3 level teaspoons
1 level tablespoon	=	15 ml
1 level teaspoon	=	5 ml

If greater accuracy is not required

1 rounded teaspoon	=	2 level teaspoons
1 heaped teaspoon	=	3 level teaspoons or 1 level tablespoon

Guide to Steaming Times for Vegetables

Type of vegetable — *Steaming time*

Type of vegetable	Steaming time
Asparagus	5–7 min
Beansprouts	3 min
Beetroot (sliced)	5–7 min
Broccoli (florets)	5–7 min
Brussels sprouts	5–7 min
Cabbage (chopped)	4–6 min
Cauliflower (florets)	5–7 min
Carrots (thickly sliced)	5–7 min
Carrots (thinly sliced)	3–5 min
Courgettes (sliced)	3–5 min
Green beans	5–7 min
Kale	3–5 min
Mangetout peas	3–5 min
Mustard greens	3–5 min
Parsnips (sliced)	5–7 min
Peas	3–5 min
Potatoes (cubed)	5–7 min
Spinach	3–5 min
Sprouting broccoli	5–7 min

Times given for steaming from when water has started to boil.

How to Play Fly Away Sparrow

The players all sit around a table and each player puts his or her right forefinger on the table. When the host says, 'Fly away, sparrow', each player has to raise his or her finger. However, if the host says, 'Fly away, mouse' or anything that does not fly, the players should not raise their fingers. The first person to make a mistake and raise a finger when it should not be raised, or fail to raise it on command, is out of the game. The game continues until all but one player remains.

STERILISING KITCHEN CLOTHS

To sterilise kitchen cloths, put them in the microwave for a couple of minutes to kill the germs. Remember when taking the cloth out of the microwave that it will be very hot, so use tongs or leave it to cool before removing it.

LASSIE COME HOME!

If your puppy or dog won't come at your command, don't chase after it! Your pet will think it's a great game and will run away faster and farther. Instead, lie down and wait. The dog will want to see what you are doing and will come to you. When it does, grab it!

Note: this is an emergency measure and not a long-term solution. Solve the problem by bringing the dog to obedience classes.

ST VALENTINE'S DAY PREDICTIONS

Apparently a young girl is able to tell what kind of man she will marry by the first bird she sees on 14 February, St Valentine's Day:

Blackbird	Clergyman or priest
Blue bird	Happy man
Crossbill	Argumentative man
Dove	Good man
Goldfinch	Rich man
Robin	Sailor
Sparrow	Farmer
Woodpecker	She will remain a spinster

ORANGES AND LEMONS

If you are making a recipe that calls for the zest of a citrus fruit, but not the juice, don't just take off the zest and leave the fruit: it will dry out quickly and you will have to throw it away. Instead, squeeze the juice out into compartments in an ice cube tray and freeze it until needed – for another recipe or to flavour a glass of water.

SYNTHETIC FABRICS AND THEIR CARE

Fabric	Use/Appearance	Care
Acetate	Normally used for linings	Hand wash in warm water and iron while damp; do not sprinkle water on the fabric or it may come out blotchy; do not use solvent stain removers
Acrylic	A substitute for fine wool	Follow care instructions; do not wash at high temperatures or the creases will never come out; if handwashing, do not wring the garment
Ciré	Has a shiny finish	Must be dry cleaned
Nylon	A strong, versatile fibre	Follow care instructions for washing; white nylon turns grey if washed in very hot water and bleach does not whiten it; a cold water rinse ensures a crease-free finish, so nylon does not usually need ironing
Polyester	Easycare woven or knitted fabric, often blended with natural fibres	Follow care instructions; and never boil; cold rinsing helps to eliminate creases; pleated fabrics should be drip dried
Viscose	Good-quality viscose that imitates a variety of natural fibres such as silk and is usually easy to care for	Wash as for wool, as it is delicate; do not iron along seams or marks will appear

GET DIVINE HELP AROUND THE HOUSE

Household job	*Patron saint*
Baking	Elizabeth of Hungary
	Nicholas of Myra
Carpentry	Joseph
	Matthias
Cooking	Lawrence
	Martha
Crafts	Dymphna
Embroidery	Clare
	Parasceva
Finding Keys	Zita
Finding Lost Objects	Anthony
Gardening	Adelard
	Christopher
	Fiacre
Housework	Zita
Knife Sharpening	Catherine of Alexandria
Laundry	Clare of Assisi
	Lawrence
Painting and Decorating	Luke
Plastering	Bartholomew
Protection against Mice	Servatus
Protection against Insects	Dominic of Silos
Sewing	Anne
Tapestry Making	Francis of Assisi

And if you are really desperate, try St Jude Thaddeus, the patron saint of Desperate Situations.

NO MORE TEARS BEFORE BEDTIME

For a remedy against hysterics, pound caraway seeds with ginger and salt and eat the paste on bread and butter before going to bed.

The Wonder of Colour

Under good light, the human eye can distinguish 10 million different colours. All these different hues are created using: red, blue, yellow, black and white.

A colour wheel shows you the relationships between different colours. Using one can help you choose colours when decorating. The cool colours (blues and greens) are on the right of the wheel, while the warm colours (oranges, reds and yellows) are on the left of the wheel. Warm colours seem to advance, while cool colours recede. Colours near each other on the wheel will look harmonious together, while colours opposite each other will give an electric jolt.

The Colour wheel

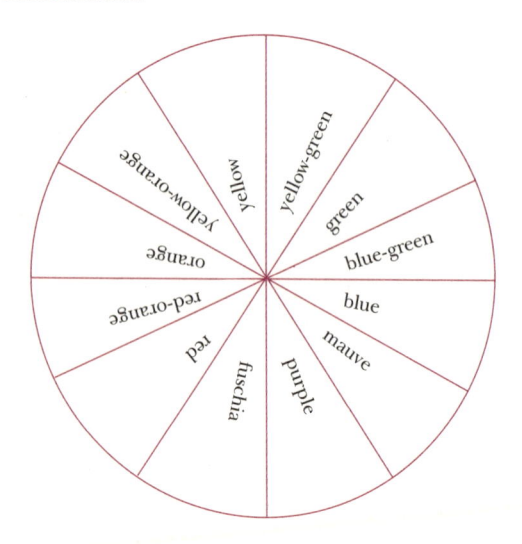

Colour Identification

Colours are divided into groups – primary, secondary, tertiary, complementary and harmonic – which are explained below.

Primary colours: Red, yellow and blue. These are the only colours that cannot be made by mixing other colours together.
Secondary colours: Violet, green, orange. These colours are created by mixing equal amounts of two primary colours.
Tertiary colours: An even mixture of a primary colour with a neighbouring secondary colour – for example, turquoise is made by mixing blue and green.
Complementary colours: These colours can be found opposite each other on the colour wheel – for example, blue and orange are complementary colours.
Harmonic colours: These colours are next to each other on the colour wheel, such as orange and golden yellow.
Shade: A colour that is made darker by adding black.
Tint: A colour that is made lighter by adding white.

Handy Hints for Using Colours

You can use colour to give a room its own distinctive atmosphere. Here are some useful hints on how to choose the right colour – or colours – and how to avoid the wrong ones.

- Using lots of different colours in the same room is jarring and makes it difficult to focus on any particular area.
- A completely neutral palette (creamy whites and beige) can be dull – you can add touches of colour to create contrast and interest.
- Too many bright colours? You can tone them down by adding accessories such as cushions in neutral colours.
- Dark floors absorb light, pale floors reflect it, so to make a room look lighter, keep the floor pale.
- Neutrals are restful; bright colours are energising.

A COMPENDIUM OF HOUSEHOLD HINTS

INDEX

Adages, household 29
Addressing people
  nobility/rank 64
  ordinary 65
  servants 113
American measures 106
Anniversaries, wedding 25
Antique furniture, British 60
Ants, getting rid of 116
Art, colour-fast 34
Banana split 6
Baths 70
Battery sizes/types 52
Beans/Pulses, soaking/cooking times 16
Beef 66
  tea 49
Beer, Belgian 8
Bees 92
Beeton's advice, Mrs 32, 51, 113
Birds, weather lore 54
Biro marks 91
Birth days 108
Birthstones 31
Biscuits, stale 100
Bleach, ecological 15
Blood, cleaning off 6
Boiling point 98
  sugar 110
Bow tie, tying a 77
Brandy snifter 104
Bread, freshening
  stale 15
  keeping it fresh 73
  long-life 34
Brooms 83
Brushes 83
  cleaning paint 68

Burnt pan, cleaning a 25
Butterscotch sundae 63
Calendar, gregorian 33
Capacity of bowls/tins 11
Car games for kids 87
Caring for carpets 39, 70, 105
  fabrics 20, 35, 84, 98, 99, 104, 120
  houseplants 45
  wood 19
Carving tips 30
Cats, top ten names 27
  and houseplants 107
Cereal, stale 100
Chair designers, modern 74
Champagne, glasses 105
  keeping it fizzy 93
Chewing gum removal 10
China, patterns 81
  packing 73
  tea 80
Chocolate, composition of 35
Chopping wood 29
Christenings 68
Christmas dinner 42–43
Cigar, smoking a 33
  types 60
Cleaning artificial flowers 99
  baths 70
  blitz 13
  blood from clothes 6
  burnt pans 25
  clothes 101
  ecologically 15, 51
  favourite screen cleaners 90
  gems 55
  grating 47
  irons 39

lampshades 57
mirrors 15
after painting 67, 68, 70
tapestry 74
trainers 108
Clothes creases 21, 95
   cleaning kit 101
   packing 21
   patching 47
   removing blood 6
   removing creases 21
   scorches on 98
Clutter busting 40
Cocktail glasses 59
   party 7
Cocktails
   classic 7
   Harvey Wallbanger 27
   Long Island Iced Tea 47
   Mai Tai 15
   Screwdriver 73
Coffee, perfect 63
   shop lingo 85
Colour, using 122–123
   wheel 122
Coloureds, washing 108
Colours, keeping bright 39
Companion planting 114
Compost, successful 82
Conversation, rules of 17
Conversion tables 9, 11, 16, 52, 58, 63, 93, 106, 107, 116
Cooking, beans/pulses 16
   beef 66
   boiling point 98
   Christmas dinner 42–43
   deep-frying 112
   fish 17
   game 58
   haybox 19

   lamb 115
   pastry 41, 69
   pork 115
   sweets 110
   temperatures 34
   turkey 74
   veal 66
   vegetables 118
Cotton care 20
   darning 18
Creases, removing 21, 95
Cuckoo, hearing the first 77
Cuffs, reshaping stretched 117
Curtains, freshening shower 89
   hanging 57
Cutlery, arranging 96
Dance floor preparation 38
Darning fabric 18
Decanter, drying a 32
Deep-frying 112
Deer repellent 27
Delicate fabrics 55, 84
Diamonds, choosing 36–37
Dimensions of baking cutters/tins 11
Dining table, laying the 96–97
Dinner, dressing for 94
Dogs, most popular breeds 62
   top ten names 6
   training 88
Drain grating, cleaning 47
Drains 108
Dressmaking terms 89
Drinker's dilemma 34
Dry cleaning 12
Dust-free spectacles 38
Ecological, bleach 15
   cleaning 51
Eggs 19
   stains on silver 57

A COMPENDIUM OF HOUSEHOLD HINTS

Etiquette, gloves 34
  wedding 76
Fabric care, cotton 20
  darning 18
  delicates 55, 84
  linen 99
  removing pet hair 113
  scorces 98
  silk 104
  synthetics 120
  wool 23
Feng Shui 48, 91
Fingernails, trimming baby's 26
Fire, laying a 71
Fish, choosing fresh 105
  grilling 117
  serving 30
  tropical 92
Fleas, fighting 21
Flower arranging 46, 96
  artificial/dried 68, 99
  meaning of 22
Freezer star symbols 98
Fruit, how to eat 102
  seasonal 56
Furniture periods 60, 74
  polish 67
Gallons 58, 107
Game 30, 58
Games, beans are hot 100
  fly away sparrow 118
  hunt the slipper 70
  kids in cars 86
Glass, packing 73
Gloves 34
Grace and deportment 49
Hairbrushes, washing 49
Hand care 19
Hanging curtains 57
  pictures 87

Harvey Wallbanger 27
Haybox cookery 19
Healthy living 25
Herbs, companion planting 114
  drying 67
  language of 38
  really useful 75
Hiccups, stopping 13
Hinges, creaky 99
Host, being a perfect 95
Housemaid's box 95
Houseplants, care of 45, 75
  keeping cats off 107
Hysterics, remedy for 121
Imperial conversions 9, 11, 52, 58, 63, 93, 106, 107, 116
Invitations, wedding 50
Iron, cleaning 39
Ironing 12, 20, 21, 39, 84, 95, 98, 104, 120
Jam making 109
Jewellery, cleaning 55
Kcal/Kjoules 16
Kitchen, essential kit 78
Lamb 115
Lampshades, cleaning 57
Lemonade 113
Lemons 19, 98, 119
Linen 99
Lipstick, removing 13
Liquid measures 106
Litres/gallons 58, 107
Long Island Iced Tea 47
Magpies, counting 94
Mai Tai cocktail 15
Mango smoothie 100
Metric conversions 9, 11, 52, 58, 63, 93, 106, 107, 116
Miles per gallon/litre 107
Mirrors, cleaning 15

Moth prevention 74
Nails, pulling out 32
Necklace, restringing a 25
   untangling 62
Nettle stings 53
Numerals, Roman 52
Nuts 87
Odours, getting rid of 10, 49
Oranges 119
Ounce, spoonfuls in an 99
Oven temperatures,
   beef 66
   game 58
   lamb 115
   pastry 41
   pork 115
   turkey 74
   veal 66
Packing, clothes 21
   glass/china 73
Painting/Decorating 28, 67
   cleaning brushes 68
   cleaning hands 70
   painting a room 14
   working with gloss 75
Pastry-making 41, 69
Patching clothes 47
Pest control 52
Pets, accidents on carpets 105
   hair on upholstery 113
   keeping off furniture 14
   top ten 44
Picture hanging 87
Poison, rat 108
Polish, making furniture 67
Pomade 32
Pork 115
Port, decanting vintage 75
   how to pass 72
Predictions, St Valentine's day 119

   weather 54, 91
Pronunciation 26
Pulses 16
Queen, taking tea with 80
   writing to 52
Rings, engagement 35
Roasting times 58, 66, 74, 115
Rodent control 52
Roman numerals 52
Saints, patron 121
Salt, too much 21
Scorches, removing 98
Screen cleaners, favourite 90
Screwdriver cocktail 73
Season, what's in 56
Sewing stitches 61
Shellfish 29
Shoe repairs 49
Shower curtains, freshening 89
Silk 18, 104
Silver, cleaning 44, 57
   superstition 13
Skin food 77
Smoothie, mango 100
   strawberry banana 94
Snifter, brandy 104
Socks, lost 107
   whitening cotton 57
Soot removal 14
Spectacles, dust-free 38
Speed conversion 63
Spoons, in an ounce 99
   measures 117
Stain removal 57, 91, 107
Stale biscuits/cereal 100
   bread 15
Static, stopping 27
Steaming times, vegetables 118
Sterilising kitchen cloths 119
Strawberry banana smoothie 94

127

A COMPENDIUM OF HOUSEHOLD HINTS

Sugar, boiling 110
Sundaes, banana split 6
   butterscotch 63
Superstition 13
Sweets making 10
   sticking together 47
Symbols, freezer star 98
   washing 12
Synthetics 120
Table, laying the 96–97
   manners 8
   wobbly legs 55
Tapestry cleaning 74
Tea, beef 49
   China/India 80
   making 24
   with the Queen 80
Tea-time, first ever 90
Temperatures, cooking 16, 34, 41, 66, 74, 110, 112, 115
Tights, holes in 26
   static in 27
Tipples, holy 91
Toenails, tidy 47
Tomato plants 67
Tool kit 79
Trainers, cleaning 108
Tropical fish for beginners 92
   Feng Shui tips 91
Turkey 30, 74
U/Non-U 111
Upholstery, removing pet hair 113

Vanilla
   perfume substitute 47
   vacuuming 100
Veal 66
Vegetables 56, 114, 118
Velvet 35
Vinegar hints 62
Wallpapering terms 73
Washing/drying, cotton 20
   delicates 55, 84
   hairbrushes 49
   silks 104
   socks 57
   symbols 12
   synthetics 120
   whites/coloureds 108
   woollens 23
Weather lore, birds 54, 91
   berries on hedgerows 91
Wedding, anniversaries 25
   etiquette 76
   invitations 50
   storing gown 102
Weights, converting 93, 116
Wellies, wet 46
Whites 57, 108
Window cleaning 10
Wine, stain removal 70
   Victorian mulled 41
Wood, chopping 29
Wool 18, 23
Zip, sticky 112

Toucan Books Ltd. have endeavoured to contact and credit all known persons holding copyright or reproduction rights in this book. If any omissions or errors have occurred, persons concerned should contact Toucan Books Ltd.